Practical Machine Learning on Databricks

Seamlessly transition ML models and MLOps on Databricks

Debu Sinha

BIRMINGHAM—MUMBAI

Practical Machine Learning on Databricks

Group Product Manager: Ali Abidi
Publishing Product Manager: Tejashwini R
Content Development Editor: Priyanka Soam
Technical Editor: Kavyashree K S
Copy Editor: Safis Editing
Project Coordinator: Farheen Fathima
Proofreader: Safis Editing
Indexer: Subalakshmi Govindhan
Production Designer: Aparna Bhagat
Marketing Coordinator: Vinishka Kalra

First published: October 2023

Production reference: 1261023

Published by Packt Publishing Ltd.
Grosvenor House
11 St Paul's Square
Birmingham
B3 1RB, UK.

ISBN 978-1-80181-203-0

www.packtpub.com

To my mother, for teaching me the invaluable lessons of persistence and self-belief,
which have been my guiding stars in completing this book.

To the committed team at Packt—Dhruv Kataria, Hemangi Lotlikar, and Priyanka Soam—thank you
for your unwavering guidance and support throughout this endeavor.

To the founders of Databricks, for not only fostering an exceptional company but also for providing me
with the opportunity to grow and learn among a community of brilliant minds.

And to the talented engineers across the globe, with whom I've had the privilege to collaborate on
architecting solutions to machine learning challenges using Databricks—you inspire me every day.

- Debu Sinha

Contributors

About the author

Debu Sinha is an experienced data science and engineering leader with deep expertise in software engineering and solutions architecture. With over 10 years in the industry, Debu has a proven track record in designing scalable software applications and big data, and machine learning systems. As lead ML specialist on the Specialist Solutions Architect team at Databricks, Debu focuses on AI/ML use cases in the cloud and serves as an expert on LLMs, ML, and MLOps. With prior experience as a start-up co-founder, Debu has demonstrated skills in team-building, scaling, and delivering impactful software solutions. An established thought leader, Debu has received multiple awards and regularly speaks at industry events.

About the reviewers

Abhinav Bhatnagar (AB), a seasoned data leader with years of expertise, excels in leading teams, governance, and strategy. He holds a master's in computer science from ASU. Currently a manager of DS&E at Databricks, AB drives data development strategies. Previously, at Truecaller and Cyr3con, he showcased his prowess in boosting revenue through data solutions and architecting AI-driven pipelines. He's been recognized with accolades such as the prestigious 40 Under 40 Data Scientists. With numerous patents and publications, Abhinav Bhatnagar stands as a remarkable figure in the data science and engineering landscape. His dedication to pushing boundaries in data science, with a wealth of experience and an innovative mindset, make him a trailblazer in tech.

Amreth Chandrasehar is a director at Informatica responsible for ML engineering, observability, and SRE teams. Over the last few years, Amreth has played a key role in cloud migration, generative AI, observability, and ML adoption at various organizations. Amreth is also co-creator of the Conducktor platform, serving T-Mobile's 100+ million customers, and a tech/customer advisory board member at various companies on observability. Amreth has also co-created and open sourced Kardio.io, a service health dashboard tool. Amreth has been invited to and spoken at several key conferences, has won several awards within the company, and was recently awarded three gold awards – Globee, Stevie, and an International Achievers' Award – for his contributions to observability and generative AI.

I would like to thank my wife (Ashwinya Mani) and my son (Athvik A) for their patience and support during my review of this book.

Table of Contents

2

Part 2: ML Pipeline Components and Implementation

3

4

Understanding MLflow Components on Databricks   63

5

Create a Baseline Model Using Databricks AutoML   77

Part 3: ML Governance and Deployment

6

Model Versioning and Webhooks   99

10

Using CI/CD to Automate Model Retraining and Redeployment   191

Preface

Designed for seasoned data scientists and developers, this book is your definitive guide to leveraging Databricks for end-to-end machine learning projects. Assuming a robust foundation in Python, statistics, machine learning life cycles, and an introductory understanding of Spark, this resource aims to transition professionals from DIY environments or other cloud platforms to the Databricks ecosystem.

Kick off your journey with a succinct overview of the machine learning landscape, followed by a deep dive into Databricks' features and the MLflow framework. Navigate through crucial elements including data preparation, model selection, and training, all while exploiting Databricks feature stores for efficient feature engineering. Employ Databricks AutoML to swiftly initiate your projects and learn how to automate model retraining and deployment via Databricks workflows.

By the close of this book, you'll be well versed in utilizing MLflow for experiment tracking, inter-team collaboration, and addressing advanced needs such as model interpretability and governance. The book is laden with practical code examples and focuses on current, generally available features, yet equips you to adapt swiftly to emerging technologies in machine learning, Databricks, and MLflow.

Who this book is for?

Written for data scientists and developers well versed in Python, statistics, and ML lifecycles, this book is your transition guide to Databricks. Ideal for those shifting from DIY or other cloud setups, it assumes introductory Spark knowledge and covers end-to-end ML workflows.

What this book covers

Chapter 1, The ML Process and Its Challenges, provides an overview of the various data science use cases across different domains. It outlines the different stages and roles involved in an ML project, from data engineering to analysis, feature engineering, and ML model training and deployment.

Chapter 2, Overview of ML on Databricks, guides you through the process of registering for a Databricks trial account and explores the machine learning features specifically designed for an ML practitioner's workspace.

Chapter 3, Utilizing the Feature Store, introduces you to the concept of a feature store. We will guide you through the process of creating feature tables using Databricks' offline feature store and demonstrate their effective utilization. Additionally, we'll discuss the advantages of employing a feature store in your machine learning workflows.

Chapter 4, Understanding MLflow Components on Databricks, helps you understand what MLflow is, its components, and the benefits of using them. We will also walk through how to register a model with the MLflow Model Registry.

Chapter 5, Create a Baseline Model Using Databricks AutoML, covers what AutoML is, why it is important, and Databricks' approach to AutoML. We will also create a baseline model with AutoML.

Chapter 6, Model Versioning and Webhooks, teaches you how to utilize the MLflow model registry to manage model versioning, transition to PROD from various stages, and use webhooks to set up alerts and monitoring.

Chapter 7, Model Deployment Approaches, covers the different options for deploying an ML model utilizing the Databricks platform.

Chapter 8, Automating ML Workflows Using Databricks Jobs, explains what Databricks jobs are and how they can be used as powerful tools to automate ML workflows. We will go over how to set up an ML training workflow using the Jobs API.

Chapter 9, Model Drift Detection and Retraining, teaches you how to detect and protect against model drift in production environments.

Chapter 10, Using CI/CD to Automate Model Retraining and Redeployment, demonstrates how to set up your Databricks ML development and deployment as a CI/CD pipeline. We will use all the concepts learned about previously in this book.

To get the most out of this book

Before diving into the hands-on activities and code examples provided in this book, it's important to be aware of the software and knowledge prerequisites. The following is a summary table outlining what you'll need:

Prerequisite	Description
Databricks Runtime	This book is tailored for Databricks Runtime 13.3 LTS for Machine Learning or above.
Python proficiency (3.x)	You should be proficient in at least Python 3.x, as the code samples are primarily written in this version.
Statistics and ML basics	A strong understanding of statistics and machine learning lifecycles is assumed.
Spark knowledge (3.0 or above)	An introductory level of familiarity with Apache Spark 3.0 or above is required, as Databricks is built on Spark.
Delta Lake features (optional)	Introductory knowledge of Delta Lake features could enhance your understanding but is not mandatory.

To fully utilize all the features and code examples described in this book, you'll need a Databricks trial account, which lasts for 14 days. We recommend planning your learning journey to complete the hands-on activities within this timeframe. If you find the platform valuable and wish to continue using it beyond the trial period, consider reaching out to your Databricks contact to set up a paid workspace.

If you are using the digital version of this book, we advise you to type the code yourself or access the code from the book's GitHub repository (a link is available in the next section). Doing so will help you avoid any potential errors related to the copying and pasting of code.

After completing this book, we highly recommend you explore the latest features in both private and public previews within the Databricks documentation. This will provide you with insights into the future trajectory of machine learning on Databricks, allowing you to remain ahead of the curve and make the most of emerging functionalities.

Download the example code files

You can download the example code files for this book from GitHub at `https://github.com/PacktPublishing/Practical-Machine-Learning-on-Databricks`. If there's an update to the code, it will be updated in the GitHub repository.

We also have other code bundles from our rich catalog of books and videos available at `https://github.com/PacktPublishing/`. Check them out!

Conventions used

There are a number of text conventions used throughout this book.

`Code in text`: Indicates code words in text, database table names, folder names, filenames, file extensions, pathnames, dummy URLs, user input, and Twitter handles. Here is an example: "In the fifth cell, we first initialize some parameters such as our existing username, `experiment_name`, which is the experiment's name that's associated with our AutoML, and the `registry_model_name`, which will be the model's name in the Model Registry."

A block of code is set as follows:

```
iris = load_iris()

X = iris.data  # Features

y = iris.target  # Labels
```

Any command-line input or output is written as follows:

```
from sklearn.datasets import load_iris  # Importing the Iris dataset
from sklearn.model_selection import train_test_split  # Importing
train_test_split function
from sklearn.linear_model import LogisticRegression  # Importing
Logistic Regression model
```

Bold: Indicates a new term, an important word, or words that you see onscreen. For instance, words in menus or dialog boxes appear in **bold**. Here is an example: "To find out which libraries are included in your runtime, you can refer to the **System Environment** subsection of the Databricks Runtime release notes to check your specific runtime version."

> **Tips or important notes**
> Appear like this.

Get in touch

Feedback from our readers is always welcome.

General feedback: If you have questions about any aspect of this book, email us at customercare@ packtpub.com and mention the book title in the subject of your message.

Errata: Although we have taken every care to ensure the accuracy of our content, mistakes do happen. If you have found a mistake in this book, we would be grateful if you would report this to us. Please visit www.packtpub.com/support/errata and fill in the form.

Piracy: If you come across any illegal copies of our works in any form on the internet, we would be grateful if you would provide us with the location address or website name. Please contact us at copyright@packt.com with a link to the material.

If you are interested in becoming an author: If there is a topic that you have expertise in and you are interested in either writing or contributing to a book, please visit authors.packtpub.com.

Reviews

Please leave a review. Once you have read and used this book, why not leave a review on the site that you purchased it from? Potential readers can then see and use your unbiased opinion to make purchase decisions, we at Packt can understand what you think about our products, and our authors can see your feedback on their book. Thank you!

For more information about Packt, please visit packtpub.com.

Share Your Thoughts

Once you've read *Practical Machine Learning on Databricks*, we'd love to hear your thoughts! Scan the QR code below to go straight to the Amazon review page for this book and share your feedback.

https://packt.link/r/1-801-81203-9

Your review is important to us and the tech community and will help us make sure we're delivering excellent quality content.

Download a free PDF copy of this book

Thanks for purchasing this book!

Do you like to read on the go but are unable to carry your print books everywhere? Is your eBook purchase not compatible with the device of your choice?

Don't worry, now with every Packt book you get a DRM-free PDF version of that book at no cost.

Read anywhere, any place, on any device. Search, copy, and paste code from your favorite technical books directly into your application.

The perks don't stop there, you can get exclusive access to discounts, newsletters, and great free content in your inbox daily

Follow these simple steps to get the benefits:

1. Scan the QR code or visit the link below

https://packt.link/free-ebook/9781801812030

2. Submit your proof of purchase

3. That's it! We'll send your free PDF and other benefits to your email directly

Part 1: Introduction

This part mainly focuses on data science use cases, the life cycle of and personas involved in a data science project (data engineers, analysts, and scientists), and the challenges of ML development in organizations.

This section has the following chapters:

- *Chapter 1, The ML Process and Its Challenges*
- *Chapter 2, Overview of ML on Databricks*

1
The ML Process and Its Challenges

Welcome to the world of simplifying your **machine learning (ML)** life cycle with the Databricks platform.

As a senior specialist solutions architect at Databricks specializing in ML, over the years, I have had the opportunity to collaborate with enterprises to architect ML-capable platforms to solve their unique business use cases using the Databricks platform. Now, that experience will be at your service to learn from. The knowledge you will gain from this book will open new career opportunities for you and change how you approach architecting ML pipelines for your organization's ML use cases.

This book does assume that you have a reasonable understanding of the Python language as the accompanying code samples will be in Python. This book is not about teaching you ML techniques from scratch; it is assumed that you are an experienced data science practitioner who wants to learn how to take your ML use cases from development to production and all the steps in the middle using the Databricks platform.

For this book, some Python and pandas know-how is required. Being familiar with Apache Spark is a plus, and having a solid grasp of ML and data science is necessary.

> **Note**
> This book focuses on the features that are currently generally available. The code examples provided utilize Databricks notebooks. While Databricks is actively developing features to support workflows using external **integrated development environments (IDEs)**, these specific features are not covered in this book. Also, going through this book will give you a solid foundation to quickly pick up new features as they become GA.

In this chapter, we will cover the following:

- Understanding the typical ML process
- Discovering the personas involved with the machine learning process in organizations

- Challenges with productionizing machine learning use cases in organizations
- Understanding the requirements of an enterprise machine learning platform
- Exploring Databricks and the Lakehouse architecture

By the end of this chapter, you should have a fundamental understanding of what a typical ML development life cycle looks like in an enterprise and the different personas involved in it. You will also know why most ML projects fail to deliver business value and how the Databricks Lakehouse Platform provides a solution.

Understanding the typical machine learning process

The following diagram summarizes the ML process in an organization:

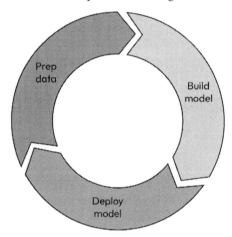

Figure 1.1 – The data science development life cycle consists of three
main stages – data preparation, modeling, and deployment

> **Note**
> Source: https://azure.microsoft.com/mediahandler/files/resourcefiles/
> standardizing-the-machine-learning-lifecycle/Standardizing%20
> ML%20eBook.pdf.

It is an iterative process. The raw structured and unstructured data first lands into a data lake from different sources. A data lake utilizes the scalable and cheap storage provided by cloud storage such as **Amazon Simple Storage Service (S3)** or **Azure Data Lake Storage (ADLS)**, depending on which cloud provider an organization uses. Due to regulations, many organizations have a multi-cloud strategy, making it essential to choose cloud-agnostic technologies and frameworks to simplify infrastructure management and reduce operational overhead.

Databricks defined a design pattern called the medallion architecture to organize data in a data lake. Before moving forward, let's briefly understand what the medallion architecture is:

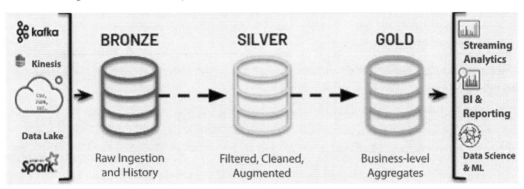

Figure 1.2 – Databricks medallion architecture

The medallion architecture is a data design pattern that's used in a Lakehouse to organize data logically. It involves structuring data into layers (Bronze, Silver, and Gold) to progressively improve its quality and structure. The medallion architecture is also referred to as a "multi-hop" architecture.

The Lakehouse architecture, which combines the best features of data lakes and data warehouses, offers several benefits, including a simple data model, ease of implementation, incremental **extract, transform, and load** (ETL), and the ability to recreate tables from raw data at any time. It also provides features such as ACID transactions and time travel for data versioning and historical analysis. We will expand more on the lakehouse in the *Exploring the Databricks Lakehouse architecture* section.

In the medallion architecture, the Bronze layer holds raw data sourced from external systems, preserving its original structure along with additional metadata. The focus here is on quick **change data capture** (**CDC**) and maintaining a historical archive. The Silver layer, on the other hand, houses cleansed, conformed, and "just enough" transformed data. It provides an enterprise-wide view of key business entities and serves as a source for self-service analytics, ad hoc reporting, and advanced analytics.

The Gold layer is where curated business-level tables reside that have been organized for consumption and reporting purposes. This layer utilizes denormalized, read-optimized data models with fewer joins. Complex transformations and data quality rules are applied here, facilitating the final presentation layer for various projects, such as customer analytics, product quality analytics, inventory analytics, and more. Traditional data marts and **enterprise data warehouses** (**EDWs**) can also be integrated into the lakehouse to enable comprehensive "pan-EDW" advanced analytics and ML.

The medallion architecture aligns well with the concept of a data mesh, where Bronze and Silver tables can be joined in a "one-to-many" fashion to generate multiple downstream tables, enhancing data scalability and autonomy.

Apache Spark has taken over Hadoop as the *de facto* standard for processing data at scale in the last six years due to advancements in performance and large-scale developer community adoption and support. There are many excellent books on Apache Spark written by the creators of Apache Spark themselves; these have been listed in the *Further reading* section. They can give more insights into the other benefits of Apache Spark.

Once the clean data lands in the Gold standard tables, features are generated by combining gold datasets, which act as input for ML model training.

During the model development and training phase, various sets of **hyperparameters** and ML algorithms are tested to identify the optimal combination of the model and corresponding hyperparameters. This process relies on predetermined evaluation metrics such as accuracy, R2 score, and F1 score.

In the context of ML, hyperparameters are parameters that govern the learning process of a model. They are not learned from the data itself but are set before training. Examples of hyperparameters include the learning rate, regularization strength, number of hidden layers in a neural network, or the choice of a kernel function in a support vector machine. Adjusting these hyperparameters can significantly impact the performance and behavior of the model.

On the other hand, training an ML model involves deriving values for other **model parameters**, such as node weights or model coefficients. These parameters are learned during the training process using the training data to minimize a chosen loss or error function. They are specific to the model being trained and are determined iteratively through optimization techniques such as gradient descent or closed-form solutions.

Expanding beyond node weights, model parameters can also include coefficients in regression models, intercept terms, feature importance scores in decision trees, or filter weights in convolutional neural networks. These parameters are directly learned from the data during the training process and contribute to the model's ability to make predictions.

> **Parameters**
>
> You can learn more about parameters at `https://en.wikipedia.org/wiki/Parameter`.

The finalized model is deployed either for batch, streaming, or real-time inference as a **Representational State Transfer (REST)** endpoint using containers. In this phase, we set up monitoring for drift and governance around the deployed models to manage the model life cycle and enforce access control around usage. Let's take a look at the different personas involved in taking an ML use case from development to production.

Discovering the roles associated with machine learning projects in organizations

Typically, three different types of persona are involved in developing an ML solution in an organization:

- **Data engineers**: The data engineers create data pipelines that take in structured, semi-structured, and unstructured data from source systems and ingest them in a data lake. Once the raw data lands in the data lake, the data engineers are also responsible for securely storing the data, ensuring that the data is reliable, clean, and easy to discover and utilize by the users in the organization.

- **Data scientists**: Data scientists collaborate with **subject matter experts** (**SMEs**) to understand and address business problems, ensuring a solid business justification for projects. They utilize clean data from data lakes and perform feature engineering, selecting and transforming relevant features. By developing and training multiple ML models with different sets of hyperparameters, data scientists can evaluate them on test sets to identify the best-performing model. Throughout this process, collaboration with SMEs validates the models against business requirements, ensuring their alignment with objectives and **key performance indicators** (**KPIs**). This iterative approach helps data scientists select a model that effectively solves the problem and meets the specified KPIs.

- **Machine learning engineers**: The ML engineering teams deploy the ML models created by data scientists into production environments. It is crucial to establish procedures, governance, and access control early on, including defining data scientist access to specific environments and data. ML engineers also implement monitoring systems to track model performance and data drift. They enforce governance practices, track model lineage, and ensure access control for data security and compliance throughout the ML life cycle.

A typical ML project life cycle consists of data engineering, then data science, and lastly, production deployment by the ML engineering team. This is an iterative process.

Now, let's take a look at the various challenges involved in productionizing ML models.

Challenges with productionizing machine learning use cases in organizations

At this point, we understand what a typical ML project life cycle looks like in an organization and the different personas involved in the ML process. It looks very intuitive, though we still see many enterprises struggling to deliver business value from their data science projects.

In 2017, Gartner analyst Nick Heudecker admitted that 85% of data science projects fail. A report published by **Dimensional Research** (https://dimensionalresearch.com/) also uncovered that only 4% of companies have been successful in deploying ML use cases to production. A recent study done by Rackspace Global Technologies in 2021 uncovered that only 20% of the 1,870 organizations in various industries have mature AI and ML practices.

> **Sources**
> See the *Further reading* section for more details on these statistics.

Most enterprises face some common technical challenges in successfully delivering business value from data science projects:

- **Unintended data silos and messy data**: Data silos can be considered as groups of data in an organization that are governed and accessible only by specific users or groups within the organization. Some valid reasons to have data silos include compliance with particular regulations around privacy laws such as **General Data Protection Regulation** (**GDPR**) in Europe or the **California Privacy Rights Act** (**CCPA**). These conditions are usually an exception to the norm. Gartner stated that almost 87% of organizations have low analytics and business intelligence maturity, meaning that data is not being fully utilized.

  Data silos generally arise as different departments within organizations. They have different technology stacks to manage and process the data.

  The following figure highlights this challenge:

Data Scientist vs. Machine Learning Engineer vs. Data Engineer

	Data scientist	Machine learning engineer	Data engineer
What they do	Build models that help business get better insights and make predictions from their data	Automate ML processes and make models work in a production environment.	Build, test and maintain data pipelines; provide ML models with quality data.
Skill set	✓ Knowledge of math and statistics ✓ Decision making and data optimization skills ✓ High proficiency in SQL ✓ Scripting skills (R/Python)	✓ Solid programming background ✓ Data science skills ✓ Knowledge of math and statistics ✓ Rapid prototyping skills ✓ Good problem-solving-skills ✓ Proficiency in deep learning frameworks	✓ Scripting skills (Linux commands) ✓ Knowledge of databases ✓ Knowledge of cloud technologies ✓ Proficiency in SQL ✓ Data modelling skills ✓ ELT development skills
Tools used	Python, R, Pandas, Jupyter notebooks, SQL	Python, PyTorch, TensorFlow, cloud services	SQL, Oracle, Hadoop, Amazon S3, Python

Figure 1.3 – The tools used by the different teams in an organization and the different silos

The different personas work with different sets of tools and have different work environments. Data analysts, data engineers, data scientists, and ML engineers utilize different tools and development environments due to their distinct roles and objectives. Data analysts rely on SQL, spreadsheets, and visualization tools for insights and reporting. Data engineers work with programming languages and platforms such as Apache Spark to build and manage data infrastructure. Data scientists use statistical programming languages, ML frameworks, and data visualization libraries to develop predictive models. ML engineers combine ML expertise with software engineering skills to deploy models into production systems. These divergent toolsets can pose challenges in terms of data consistency, tool compatibility, and collaboration. Standardized processes and knowledge sharing can help mitigate these challenges and foster effective teamwork. Traditionally, there is little to no collaboration between these teams. As a result, a data science use case with a validated business value may not be developed at the required pace, negatively impacting the growth and effective management of the business.

When the concept of data lakes came up in the past decade, they promised a scalable and cheap solution to support structured and unstructured data. The goal was to enable organization-wide effective usage and collaboration of data. In reality, most data lakes ended up becoming data swamps, with little to no governance regarding the quality of data.

This inherently made ML very difficult since an ML model is only as good as the data it's trained on.

- **Building and managing an effective ML production environment is challenging**: The ML teams at Google have done a lot of research on the technical challenges around setting up an ML development environment. A research paper published in NeurIPS on hidden technical debt in ML systems engineering from Google (`https://proceedings.neurips.cc/paper/2015/file/86df7dcfd896fcaf2674f757a2463eba-Paper.pdf`) documented that writing ML code is just a tiny piece of the whole ML development life cycle. To develop an effective ML development practice in an organization, many tools, configurations, and monitoring aspects need to be integrated into the overall architecture. One of the critical components is monitoring drift in model performance and providing feedback and retraining:

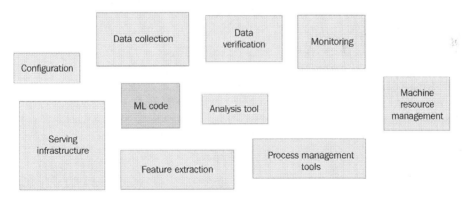

Figure 1.4 – Hidden Technical Debt in Machine Learning Systems, NeurIPS 2015

Let's understand the requirements of an enterprise-grade ML platform a bit more.

Understanding the requirements of an enterprise-grade machine learning platform

In the fast-paced world of **artificial intelligence** (**AI**) and ML, an enterprise-grade ML platform takes center stage as a critical component. It is a comprehensive software platform that offers the infrastructure, tools, and processes required to construct, deploy, and manage ML models at a grand scale. However, a truly robust ML platform goes beyond these capabilities, extending to every stage of the ML life cycle, from data preparation, model training, and deployment to constant monitoring and improvements.

When we speak of an enterprise-grade ML platform, several key attributes determine its effectiveness, each of which is considered a cornerstone of such platforms. Let's delve deeper into each of these critical requirements and understand their significance in an enterprise setting.

Scalability – the growth catalyst

Scalability is an essential attribute, enabling the platform to adapt to the expanding needs of a burgeoning organization. In the context of ML, this encompasses the capacity to handle voluminous datasets, manage multiple models simultaneously, and accommodate a growing number of concurrent users. As the organization's data grows exponentially, the platform must have the capability to expand and efficiently process the increasing data without compromising performance.

Performance – ensuring efficiency and speed

In a real-world enterprise setting, the ML platform's performance directly influences business operations. It should possess the capability to deliver high performance both in the training and inference stages. These stages are critical to ensure that models can be efficiently trained with minimum resources, and then deployed into production environments, ready to make timely and accurate predictions. A high-performance platform translates to faster decisions, and in today's fast-paced business world, every second counts.

Security – safeguarding data and models

In an era where data breaches are common, an ML platform's security becomes a paramount concern. A robust ML platform should prioritize security and comply with industry regulations. This involves an assortment of features such as stringent data encryption techniques, access control mechanisms to prevent unauthorized access, and auditing capabilities to track activities in the system, all of which contribute to securely handling sensitive data and ML models.

Governance – steering the machine learning life cycle

Governance is an often overlooked yet vital attribute of an enterprise-grade ML platform. Effective governance tools can facilitate the management of the entire life cycle of ML models. They can control versioning, maintain lineage tracking to understand the evolution of models, and audit for regulatory compliance and transparency. As the complexity of ML projects increases, governance tools ensure smooth sailing by managing the models and maintaining a clean and understandable system.

Reproducibility – ensuring trust and consistency

Reproducibility serves as a foundation for trust in any ML model. The ML platform should ensure the reproducibility of the results from ML experiments, thereby establishing credibility and confidence in the models. This means that given the same data and the same conditions, the model should produce the same outputs consistently. Reproducibility directly impacts the decision-making process, ensuring the decisions are consistent and reliable, and the models can be trusted.

Ease of use – balancing complexity and usability

Last, but by no means least, is the ease of use of the ML platform. Despite the inherent complexity of ML processes, the platform should be intuitive and user-friendly for a wide range of users, from data scientists to ML engineers. This extends to features such as a streamlined user interface, a well-documented API, and a user-centric design, making it easier for users to develop, deploy, and manage models. An easy-to-use platform reduces the barriers to entry, increases adoption, and empowers users to focus more on the ML tasks at hand rather than struggling with the platform.

In essence, an enterprise MLOps platform needs capabilities for model development, deployment, scalability, collaboration, monitoring, and automation. Databricks fits in by offering a unified environment for ML practitioners to develop and train models, deploy them at scale, and monitor their performance. It supports collaboration, integrates with popular deployment technologies, and provides automation and CI/CD capabilities.

Now, let's delve deeper into the capabilities of the Databricks Lakehouse architecture and its unified AI/analytics platform, which establish it as an exceptional ML platform for enterprise readiness.

Exploring Databricks and the Lakehouse architecture

Databricks is a renowned cloud-native and enterprise-ready data analytics platform that integrates data engineering, data science, and ML to enable organizations to develop and deploy ML models at scale.

Cloud-native refers to an approach where software applications are designed, developed, and deployed specifically for cloud environments. It involves utilizing technologies such as containers, microservices, and orchestration platforms to achieve scalability, resilience, and agility. By leveraging the cloud's capabilities, Databricks can scale dynamically, recover from failures, and adapt quickly to changing demands, enabling organizations to maximize the benefits of cloud computing.

Databricks achieves the six cornerstones of an enterprise-grade ML platform. Let's take a closer look.

Scalability – the growth catalyst

Databricks provides fully managed Apache Spark (an open source distributed computing system known for its ability to handle large volumes of data and perform computations in a distributed manner) clusters.

Apache Spark consists of several components, including nodes and a driver program. **Nodes** refer to the individual machines or servers within the Spark cluster that contribute computational resources. The **driver** program is responsible for running the user's application code and coordinating the overall execution of the Spark job. It communicates with the **cluster manager** to allocate resources and manages the **SparkContext**, which serves as the entry point to the Spark cluster. **RDDs** are the core data structure, enabling parallel processing, and Spark uses a **directed acyclic graph** (**DAG**) to optimize computations. **Transformations** and **actions** are performed on RDDs, while cluster managers handle resource allocation. Additionally, caching and shuffling enhance performance.

The **DataFrames** API in Spark is a distributed collection of data that's organized into named columns. It provides a higher-level abstraction compared to working directly with RDDs in Spark, making it easier to manipulate and analyze structured data. It supports a SQL-like syntax and provides a wide range of functions for data manipulation and transformation.

Spark provides APIs in various languages, including Scala, Java, Python, and R, allowing users to leverage their existing skills and choose the language they are most comfortable with.

Apache Spark processes large datasets across multiple nodes, making it highly scalable. It supports both streaming and batch processing. This means that you can use Spark to process real-time data streams as well as large-scale batch jobs. Spark Structured Streaming, a component of Spark, allows you to process live data streams in a scalable and fault-tolerant manner. It provides high-level abstractions that make it easy to write streaming applications using familiar batch processing concepts.

Furthermore, Databricks allows for dynamic scaling and autoscaling of clusters, which adjusts resources based on the workload, ensuring the efficient use of resources while accommodating growing organizational needs.

While this book doesn't delve into Apache Spark in detail, we have curated a *Further reading* section with excellent recommendations that will help you explore Apache Spark more comprehensively.

Performance – ensuring efficiency and speed

Databricks Runtime is optimized for the cloud and includes enhancements over open source Apache Spark that significantly increase performance. The Databricks Delta engine provides fast query execution for big data and AI workflows while reducing the time and resources needed for data preparation and iterative model training. Its optimized runtime improves both model training and inference speeds, resulting in more efficient operations.

Security – safeguarding data and models

Databricks ensures a high level of security through various means. It offers data encryption at rest and in transit, uses **role-based access control** (**RBAC**) to provide fine-grained user permissions, and integrates with identity providers for **single sign-on** (**SSO**).

Databricks also has a feature called Unity Catalog. Unity Catalog is a centralized metadata store for Databricks workspaces that offers data governance capabilities such as access control, auditing, lineage, and data discovery. Its key features include centralized governance, a universal security model, automated lineage tracking, and easy data discovery. Its benefits include improved governance, reduced operational overhead, and increased data agility. Unity Catalog is a powerful tool for enhancing data governance in Databricks. Unity Catalog is a complex topic that will not be covered extensively in this book. However, you can find more information on it in the *Further reading* section, where a link has been provided.

The Databricks platform is compliant with several industry regulations, including GDPR, CCPA, HIPAA, SOC 2 Type II, and ISO/IEC 27017. For a complete list of certifications, check out `https://www.databricks.com/trust/compliance`.

Governance – steering the machine learning life cycle

Databricks provides MLflow, an open source platform for managing the ML life cycle, including experimentation, reproducibility, and deployment. It supports model versioning and model registry for tracking model versions and their stages in the life cycle (staging, production, and others). Additionally, the platform provides audit logs for tracking user activity, helping meet regulatory requirements and promoting transparency. Databricks has its own hosted feature store as well, which we will cover in more detail in later chapters.

Reproducibility – ensuring trust and consistency

With MLflow, Databricks ensures the reproducibility of ML models. MLflow allows users to log parameters, metrics, and artifacts for each run of an experiment, providing a record of what was done and allowing for exact replication of the results. It also supports packaging code into reproducible runs and sharing it with others, further ensuring the repeatability of experiments.

Ease of use – balancing complexity and usability

Databricks provides a collaborative workspace that enables data scientists and engineers to work together seamlessly. It offers interactive notebooks with support for multiple languages (Python, R, SQL, and Scala) in a single notebook, allowing users to use their preferred language. The platform's intuitive interface, coupled with extensive documentation and a robust API, makes it user-friendly, enabling users to focus more on ML tasks rather than the complexities of platform management. In addition to its collaborative and analytical capabilities, Databricks integrates with various data sources, storage systems, and cloud platforms, making it flexible and adaptable to different data ecosystems. It supports seamless integration with popular data lakes, databases, and cloud storage services, enabling users to easily access and process data from multiple sources. Although this book specifically focuses on the ML and MLOps capabilities of Databricks, it makes sense to understand what the Databricks Lakehouse architecture is and how it simplifies scaling and managing ML project life cycles for organizations.

Lakehouse, as a term, is a combination of two terms: **data lakes** and **data warehouses**. Data warehouses are great at handling structured data and SQL queries. They are extensively used for powering **business intelligence** (**BI**) applications but have limited support for ML. They store data in proprietary formats and can only be accessed using SQL queries.

Data lakes, on the other hand, do a great job supporting ML use cases. A data lake allows organizations to store a large amount of their structured and unstructured data in a central scalable store. They are easy to scale and support open formats. However, data lakes have a significant drawback when it comes to running BI workloads. Their performance is not comparable to data warehouses. The lack of schema governance enforcement turned most data lakes in organizations into swamps.

Typically, in modern enterprise architecture, there is a need for both. This is where Databricks defined the Lakehouse architecture. Databricks provides a unified analytics platform called the Databricks Lakehouse Platform. The Lakehouse Platform provides a persona-based single platform that caters to all the personas involved in data processing and gains insights. The personas include data engineers, BI analysts, data scientists, and MLOps. This can tremendously simplify the data processing and analytics architecture of any organization.

At the time of writing this book, the Lakehouse Platform is available on all three major clouds: **Amazon Web Services** (**AWS**), **Microsoft Azure**, and **Google Compute Platform** (**GCP**).

Lakehouse can be thought of as a technology that combines data warehouses' performance and data governance aspects and makes them available at the scale of data lakes. Under the hood, Lakehouse uses an open protocol called **Delta** (`https://delta.io/`).

The Delta format adds reliability, performance, and governance to the data in data lakes. Delta also provides **Atomicity, Consistency, Isolation, and Durability** (**ACID**) transactions, making sure that all data operations either fully succeed or fail. In addition to ACID transaction support, under the hood, Delta uses the Parquet format. Unlike the regular Parquet format, the Delta format keeps track of transaction logs, offering enhanced capabilities. It also supports granular access controls to your data, along with versioning and the ability to roll back to previous versions. Delta format tables scale effortlessly with data and are underpinned by Apache Spark while utilizing advanced indexing and caching to improve performance at scale. There are many more benefits that the Delta format provides that you can read about on the official website.

When we say **Delta Lake**, we mean a data lake that uses the Delta format to provide the previously described benefits to the data lake.

The Databricks Lakehouse architecture is built on the foundation of Delta Lake:

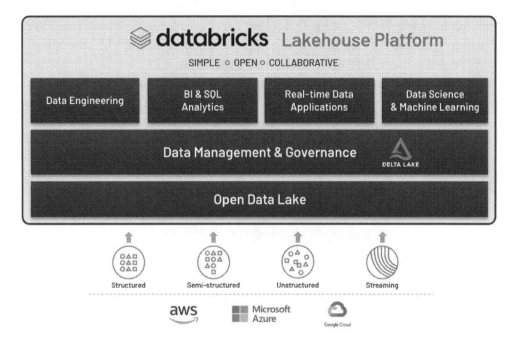

Figure 1.5 – Databricks Lakehouse Platform

> **Note**
> Source: Courtesy of Databricks

Next, let's discuss how the Databricks Lakehouse architecture can simplify ML.

Simplifying machine learning development with the Lakehouse architecture

As we saw in the previous section, the Databricks Lakehouse Platform provides a cloud-native enterprise-ready solution that simplifies the data processing needs of an organization. It provides a single platform that enables different teams across enterprises to collaborate and reduces time to market for new projects.

The Lakehouse Platform has many components specific to data scientists and ML practitioners; we will cover these in more detail later in this book. For instance, at the time of writing this book, the Lakehouse Platform released a drop-down button that allows users to switch between persona-based views. There are tabs to quickly access the fully integrated and managed feature store, model registry, and MLflow tracking server in the ML practitioner persona view:

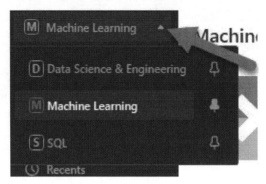

Figure 1.6 – Databricks Lakehouse Platform persona selection dropdown

With that, let's summarize this chapter.

Summary

In this chapter, we learned about ML, including the ML process, the personas involved, and the challenges organizations face in productionizing ML models. Then, we learned about the Lakehouse architecture and how the Databricks Lakehouse Platform can potentially simplify MLOps for organizations. These topics give us a solid foundation to develop a more profound understanding of how different Databricks ML-specific tools fit in the ML life cycle.

For in-depth learning about the various features and staying up to date with announcements, the Databricks documentation is the ideal resource. You can access the documentation via the link provided in the *Further reading* section. Moreover, on the documentation page, you can easily switch to different cloud-specific documentation to explore platform-specific details and functionalities.

In the next chapter, we will dive deeper into the ML-specific features of the Databricks Lakehouse Platform.

Further reading

To learn more about the topics that were covered in this chapter, take a look at the following resources:

- Wikipedia, *Hyperparameter (machine learning)* (`https://en.wikipedia.org/wiki/Hyperparameter_(machine_learning)`).

- Matt Asay, 2017, *85% of big data projects fail*, TechRepublic, November (`https://www.techrepublic.com/article/85-of-big-data-projects-fail-but-your-developers-can-help-yours-succeed/`).

- Rackspace Technologies, *New Global Rackspace Technology Study Uncovers Widespread Artificial Intelligence and Machine Learning Knowledge Gap*, January 2021 (`https://www.rackspace.com/newsroom/new-global-rackspace-technology-study-uncovers-widespread-artificial-intelligence-and`).

- Gartner, *Gartner Data Shows 87 Percent of Organizations Have Low BI and Analytics Maturity*, December 2018 (`https://www.gartner.com/en/newsroom/press-releases/2018-12-06-gartner-data-shows-87-percent-of-organizations-have-low-bi-and-analytics-maturity`).

- *Learning Spark: Lightning-Fast Data Analytics*, by Holden Karau, Andy Konwinski, Patrick Wendell, and Matei Zaharia: This comprehensive guide covers the fundamentals of Spark, including RDDs, the DataFrame API, Spark Streaming, MLlib, and GraphX. With practical examples and use cases, it will help you become proficient in using Spark for data analytics.

- *Spark: The Definitive Guide*, by Bill Chambers and Matei Zaharia: This acclaimed book provides a deep dive into Spark's core concepts and advanced features. It covers Spark's architecture, data processing techniques, ML, graph processing, and deployment considerations. Suitable for beginners and experienced users, it offers a comprehensive understanding of Spark.

- *High Performance Spark: Best Practices for Scaling and Optimizing Apache Spark*, by Holden Karau, Rachel Warren, and Matei Zaharia: This book explores strategies for optimizing Spark applications to achieve maximum performance and scalability. It offers insights into tuning Spark configurations, improving data locality, leveraging advanced features, and designing efficient data pipelines.

- *Spark in Action*, by Jean-Georges Perrin: This practical guide takes you through the entire Spark ecosystem, covering data ingestion, transformation, ML, real-time processing, and integration with other technologies. With hands-on examples and real-world use cases, it enables you to apply Spark to your specific projects.

- *Get Started using Unity Catalog* (`https://docs.databricks.com/data-governance/unity-catalog/get-started.html`)

- *Databricks documentation* (`https://docs.databricks.com/introduction/index.html`).

2
Overview of ML on Databricks

This chapter will give you a fundamental understanding of how to get started with ML on Databricks. The ML workspace is data scientist-friendly and allows rapid ML development by providing out-of-the-box support for popular ML libraries such as TensorFlow, PyTorch, and many more.

We will cover setting up a trial Databricks account and learn about the various ML-specific features available at ML practitioners' fingertips in the Databricks workspace. You will learn how to start a cluster on Databricks and create a new notebook.

In this chapter, we will cover these main topics:

- Setting up a Databricks trial account
- Introduction to the ML workspace on Databricks
- Exploring the workspace
- Exploring clusters
- Exploring notebooks
- Exploring data
- Exploring experiments
- Discovering the feature store
- Discovering the model registry
- Libraries

These topics will cover the essential features to perform effective **ML Operations (MLOps)** on Databricks. Links to the Databricks official documentation will also be included at relevant places if you wish to learn about a particular feature in more detail.

Let's look at how we can get access to a Databricks workspace.

Technical requirements

For this chapter, you'll need access to the Databricks workspace with cluster creation privileges. By default, the owner of the workspace has permission to create clusters. We will cover clusters in more detail in the *Exploring clusters* sections. You can read more about the various cluster access control options here: `https://docs.databricks.com/security/access-control/cluster-acl.html`.

Setting up a Databricks trial account

At the time of writing, Databricks is available on all the major cloud platforms, namely **Google Cloud Platform (GCP)**, **Microsoft Azure**, and **Amazon Web Services (AWS)**.

Databricks provides an easy way to either create an account within the community edition or start a 14-day trial with all the enterprise features available in the workspace.

To fully leverage the code examples provided in this book and explore the enterprise features we'll cover, I highly recommend taking advantage of the 14-day trial option. This trial will grant you access to all the necessary functionalities, ensuring a seamless experience throughout your learning journey.

Please go through this link to sign up for trial account: `https://www.databricks.com/try-databricks?itm_data=PricingPage-Trial#account`

On filling out the introductory form, you will be redirected to a page that will provide you with options to start with trial deployments on either of the three clouds or create a Community Edition account:

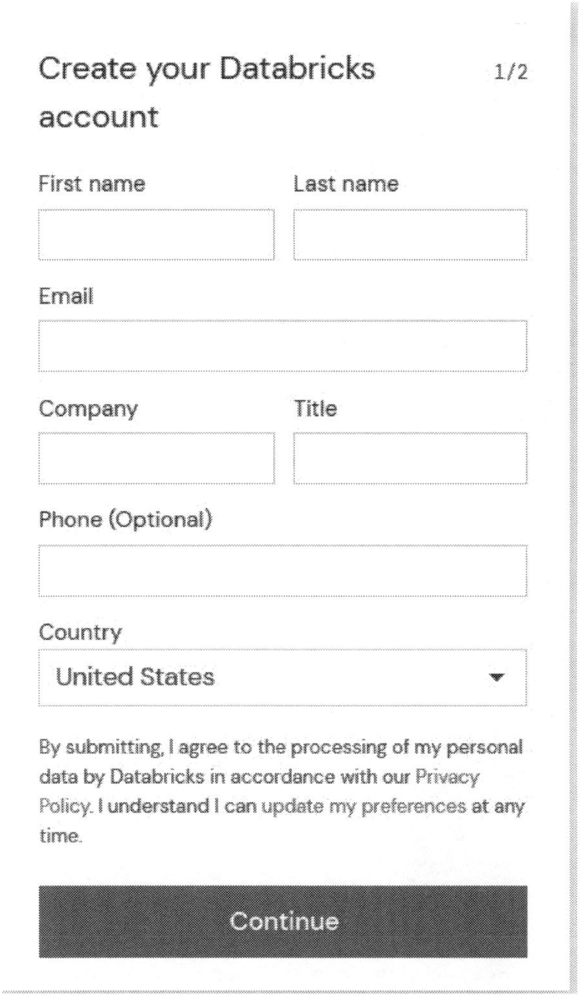

Figure 2.1 – How to get a free Databricks trial account

Once your signup is successful, you will receive an email describing how to log in to the Databricks workspace.

> **Note**
> Most of the features we will cover in this chapter will be accessible with the 14-day trial option.

Once you log into the workspace, access the persona selector tab on the left navigation bar. We will change our persona to **Machine Learning**:

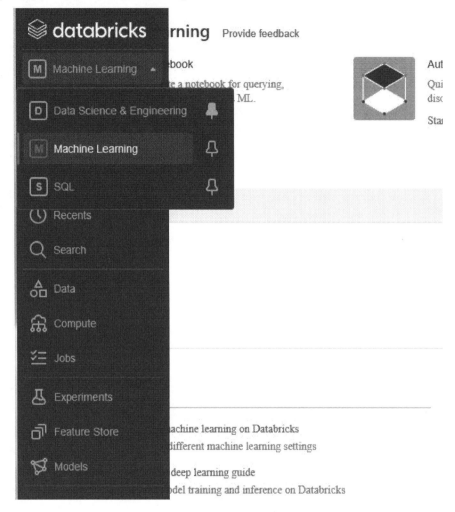

Figure 2.2 – The persona-based workspace switcher

Now, let's take a look at the new Databricks ML workspace features.

Exploring the workspace

The **workspace** is within a Databricks ML environment. Each user of the Databricks ML environment will have a workspace. Users can create notebooks and develop code in isolation or collaborate with other teammates through granular access controls. You will be working within the workspace or repos for most of your time in the Databricks environment. We will learn more about repos in the *Repos* section:

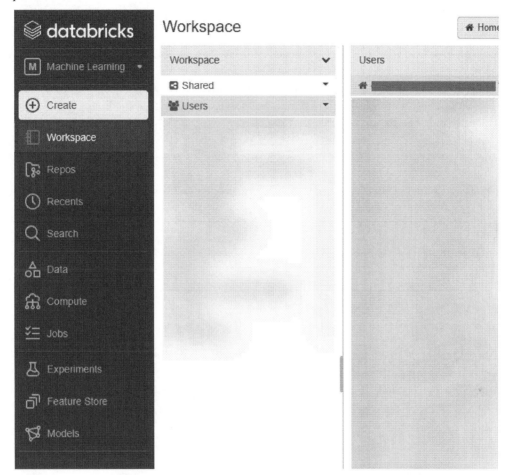

Figure 2.3 – The Workspace tab

It's important to note that the **Workspace** area is primarily intended for Databricks notebooks. While the workspace does support version control for notebooks using Git providers within Databricks, it's worth highlighting that this version control capability within workspace notebooks is now considered less recommended compared to using repos.

Version control, in the context of software development, is a system that helps track changes made to files over time. It allows you to maintain a historical record of modifications, enabling collaboration, bug tracking, and reverting to previous versions if needed. In the case of Databricks, version control specifically refers to tracking changes made to notebooks.

To enhance best practices, Databricks is transitioning away from relying solely on the version control feature within the workspace. Instead, it emphasizes the use of repos, which offers improved support for both Databricks and non-Databricks-specific files. This strategic shift provides a more comprehensive and versatile approach to managing code and files within the Databricks environment.

By utilizing repos, you can effectively manage and track changes not only to notebooks but also to other file types. This includes code files, scripts, configuration files, and more. Repos leverage popular version control systems such as Git, enabling seamless collaboration, branch management, code review workflows, and integration with external tools and services. Let's look at the **Repos** feature, which was recently added to the workspace.

Repos

Repos is short for repository. This convenient feature allows you to version control your code in the Databricks environment. Using repos, you can store arbitrary files within a Git repository. At the time of writing, Databricks supports the following Git providers:

- GitHub

- Bitbucket

- GitLab

- Azure DevOps

Databricks repos provide a logging mechanism to track and record various user interactions with a Git repository. These interactions include actions such as committing code changes and submitting pull requests. The repo features are also available through the REST **application programming interface (API)** (`https://docs.databricks.com/dev-tools/api/latest/repos.html`).

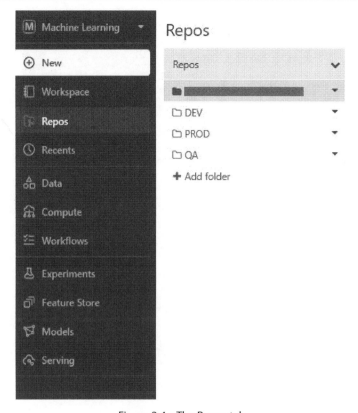

Figure 2.4 – The Repos tab

You can read more about how to set up repos for your environment at `https://docs.databricks.com/repos.html#configure-your-git-integration-with-databricks`. Repositories are essential for setting up your CI/CD processes in the Databricks environment. The **Repos** feature allows users to version their code and also allows reproducibility.

Continuous integration/continuous deployment (CI/CD) is a software development approach that involves automating the processes of integrating code changes, testing them, and deploying them to production environments. In the last chapter of this book, we will discuss more about the deployment paradigms in Databricks and CI/CD as part of your MLOps:

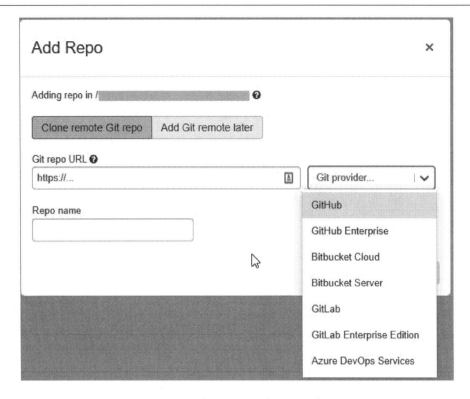

Figure 2.5 – The supported Git providers

Now, let's look at clusters, the central compute units for performing model training in the Databricks environment.

Exploring clusters

Clusters are the primary computing units that will do the heavy lifting when you're training your ML models. The VMs associated with a cluster are provisioned in Databricks users' cloud subscriptions; however, the Databricks UI provides an interface to control the cluster type and its settings.

Clusters are ephemeral compute resources. No data is stored on clusters:

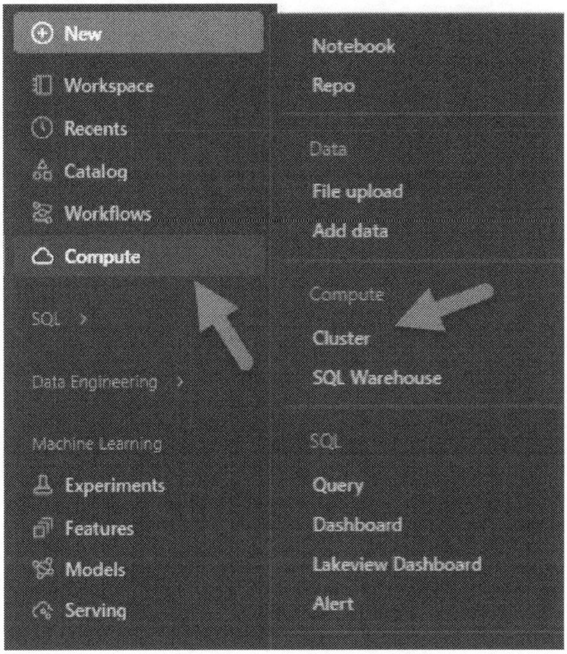

Figure 2.6 – The Clusters tab

The **Pools** feature allows end users to create Databricks VM pools. One of the benefits of working in the cloud environment is that you can request new compute resources on demand. The end user pays by the second and returns the compute once the load on the cluster is low. This is great; however, requesting a VM from the cloud provider, ramping it up, and adding it to a cluster still takes some time. Using pools, you can pre-provision VMs to keep them in a standby state. If a cluster requests new nodes and has access to the pool, then if the pool has the required VMs available, within seconds, these nodes will be added to the cluster, helping reduce the cluster scale uptime. Once the cluster is done processing high load or is terminated, the machine borrowed from the pool is returned to the pool and can be used by the next cluster. More about pools can be found here: `https://docs.databricks.com/clusters/instance-pools/index.html`.

Databricks **jobs** allow users to automate code execution on a particular schedule. It has a lot of other valuable configurations around how many times you can retry code execution in case of failure and can set up alerts in case of failure. You can read a lot more about jobs here: `https://docs.databricks.com/data-engineering/jobs/jobs-quickstart.html`. This link is for a Databricks workspace deployed on AWS; however, you can click on the **Change cloud** tab to match your deployment:

Figure 2.7 – The dropdown for selecting documentation pertinent to your cloud

For now, let's focus on the **Create Cluster** tab.

If you are coming from an ML background where most of the work has been done on your laptop or a single isolated VM, then Databricks provides an easy way to get started by providing a single-node mode. In this case, you will get all the benefits of Databricks while working on a single-node cluster. The existing non-distributed code should run as is on this cluster. As an example, the following code will run only on the driver node as is in a non-distributed manner:

```
from sklearn.datasets import load_iris  # Importing the Iris dataset
from sklearn.model_selection import train_test_split  # Importing
train_test_split function
from sklearn.linear_model import LogisticRegression  # Importing
Logistic Regression model
from sklearn.metrics import accuracy_score  # Importing accuracy_score
metric

# Load the Iris dataset
iris = load_iris()
X = iris.data  # Features
y = iris.target  # Labels
```

```
# Split the dataset into training and test sets
X_train, X_test, y_train, y_test = train_test_split(X, y, test_
size=0.2, random_state=42)

# Initialize the logistic regression model
model = LogisticRegression()

# Train the model
model.fit(X_train, y_train)

# Make predictions on the test set
y_pred = model.predict(X_test)

# Calculate the accuracy of the model
accuracy = accuracy_score(y_test, y_pred)
print("Accuracy:", accuracy)
```

> **Note**
>
> Typically, a cluster refers to a collection of machines processing data in a distributed fashion. In the case of a single-node cluster, a single **VM** runs all the processes on multiple VMs in a regular cluster.

It is straightforward to start up a cluster in the Databricks environment. All the code provided in this book can be run on a single-node cluster. To spin up a single-node cluster, follow these steps:

1. Give a name to the cluster.
2. Change the cluster mode to **Single Node**.
3. Set the latest ML runtime to **Databricks Runtime Version**.

4. Click **Create cluster**:

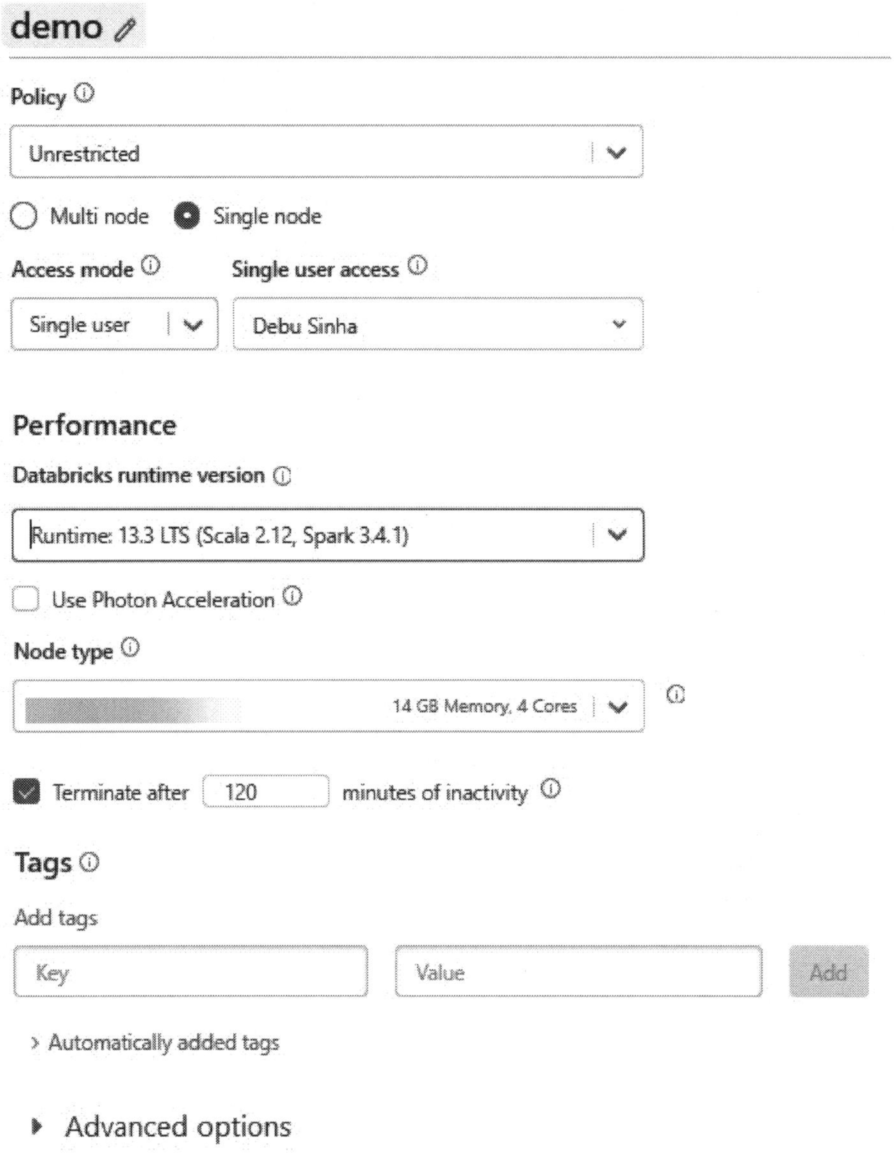

demo ✏️

Policy ⓘ

Unrestricted	⌄

◯ Multi node   ⬤ Single node

Access mode ⓘ   **Single user access** ⓘ

Single user	⌄

Debu Sinha	⌄

Performance

Databricks runtime version ⓘ

Runtime: 13.3 LTS (Scala 2.12, Spark 3.4.1)	⌄

☐ Use Photon Acceleration ⓘ

Node type ⓘ

	14 GB Memory, 4 Cores	⌄	ⓘ

☑ Terminate after [120] minutes of inactivity ⓘ

Tags ⓘ

Add tags

Key	Value	Add

> Automatically added tags

▶ Advanced options

Figure 2.8 – The New Cluster screen

This will start the process of provisioning our cluster. There are some advanced settings, such as adding tags, using init scripts, and connecting through JDBC to this cluster, that you can read about.

Databricks Runtime is a powerful platform that enhances big data analytics by improving the performance, security, and usability of Spark jobs. With features such as optimized I/O, enhanced security, and simplified operations, it offers a comprehensive solution. It comes in various flavors, including **ML** and **Photon**, catering to specific needs. Databricks Runtime is the ideal choice for running big data analytics workloads effectively. Databricks Runtime is powered by Delta Lake, which seamlessly integrates batch and streaming data to enable near-real-time analytics. Delta Lake's capability to track data versions over time is crucial for reproducing ML model training and experimentation. This ensures data consistency and empowers reproducibility in your workflows. You can read more about Databricks Runtime here: `https://docs.databricks.com/runtime/index.html`.

You will be using the ML runtime as an ML practitioner on Databricks. Databricks Runtime ML is a pre-built ML infrastructure that's integrated with the capabilities of the Databricks workspace. It provides popular ML libraries such as TensorFlow and PyTorch, distributed training libraries such as Horovod, and pre-configured GPU support. With faster cluster creation and compatibility with installed libraries, it simplifies scaling ML and deep learning tasks. Additionally, it offers data exploration, cluster management, code and environment management, automation support, and integrated MLflow for model development and deployment.

Databricks provides three different cluster access modes and their specific recommended use case patterns. All these cluster access modes can be used either in a multi-node (your cluster has a dedicated driver node and one or more executor nodes) or a single-node fashion (your cluster has a single node; both the driver program and executor programs run on a single node).

Single user

This mode is recommended for single users and data applications that can be developed using Python, Scala, SQL, and R. Clusters are set to terminate after 120 minutes of inactivity, and the standard cluster is the default cluster mode. End users can also use this cluster to execute a notebook through a Databricks job using a scheduled activity. It is best to segregate different data processing pipelines into separate standard clusters. Segregating data pipelines prevents the failure of one cluster from affecting another. As Databricks charges customers by the second, this approach is viable and widely used. A cluster with this access type supports ML workloads.

Shared

This mode is ideal when multiple users try to use the same cluster. It can provide maximum resource utilization and has lower query latency requirements in multiuser scenarios. Data applications can be developed using Python and SQL but not R and Scala. These clusters provide user isolation and also support ML workloads.

No isolation shared

This type of cluster is intended only for admin users. We won't cover too much about this type of access as this cluster type doesn't support ML use cases.

You can read more about user isolation here: `https://docs.databricks.com/notebooks/notebook-isolation.html`.

Let's take a look at single-node clusters as this is the type of cluster you will be using to run the code that's been shared as part of this book.

Single-node clusters

Single-node clusters do not have worker nodes, and all the Python code runs on the driver node. These clusters are configured to terminate after 120 minutes of inactivity by default and can be used to build and test small data pipelines and do lightweight **exploratory data analysis** (**EDA**) and ML development. Python, Scala, SQL, and R are supported.

If you want to use specific libraries not included in the runtime, we will explore the various options to install the required libraries in the *Library* section of this chapter.

Exploring notebooks

If you are familiar with **Jupyter** and **IPython notebooks**, then Databricks notebooks will look very familiar. A Databricks notebook development environment consists of cells where end users can interactively write code in R, Python, Scala, or SQL.

Databricks notebooks also have additional functionalities such as integration with the Spark UI, powerful integrated visualizations, version control, and an MLflow model tracking server. We can also parameterize a notebook and pass parameters to it at execution time.

We will cover notebooks in more detail as the code examples presented to you in this book utilize the Databricks notebook environment. Additional details about notebooks can be found at `https://docs.databricks.com/notebooks/index.html`:

Figure 2.9 – Databricks notebooks

Let's take a look at the next feature on the **Data** tab, also called the Databricks metastore.

Exploring data

By default, when a new workspace is deployed, it comes with a managed Hive **metastore**. A metastore allows you to register datasets in various formats such as **Comma-Separated Values (CSV)**, **Parquet**, **Delta format**, **text**, or **JavaScript Object Notation (JSON)** as an external table (`https://docs.databricks.com/data/metastores/index.html`). We will not go too much into detail about the metastore here:

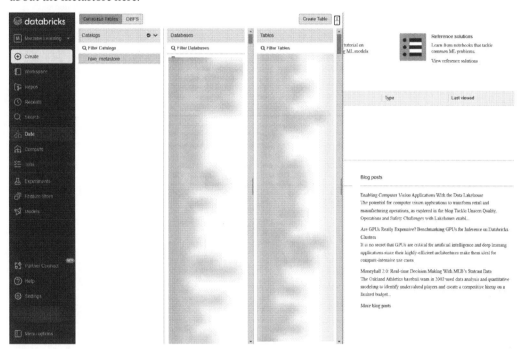

Figure 2.10 – The Data tab

It's all right if you are not familiar with the term metastore. In simple terms, it is similar to a relational database. In relational databases, there are databases and then table names and schemas. The end user can use SQL to interact with the data stored in databases and tables. Similarly, in Databricks, end users can decide to register datasets stored in cloud storage so that they're available as tables. You can learn more here: `https://docs.databricks.com/spark/latest/spark-sql/language-manual/index.html`.

The Hive metastore provides a means of implementing access control by utilizing table access control lists for local users within the workspace. However, to enhance data access governance and ensure unified control over various assets such as deployed models and AI assets, Databricks has introduced Unity Catalog as a best practice solution. This enables comprehensive management and governance across multiple workspaces.

Let's understand Unity Catalog in a bit more detail.

Unity Catalog is a unified governance solution for data and AI assets on the lakehouse. It provides centralized access control, auditing, lineage, and data discovery capabilities across Databricks workspaces:

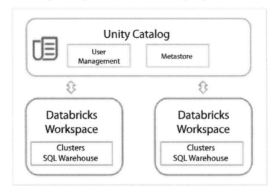

Figure 2.11 – Unity Catalog's relationship to workspaces

Here are some of the key features of Unity Catalog:

- **Define once, secure everywhere**: Unity Catalog administers data access policies across all workspaces and personas from a single place

- **Standards-compliant security model**: Unity Catalog's security model is based on standard ANSI SQL and allows administrators to grant permissions in their existing data lake

- **Built-in auditing and lineage**: Unity Catalog captures user-level audit logs and lineage data, tracking how data assets are created and used across all languages and personas

- **Data discovery**: Unity Catalog provides a search interface to help data consumers find data and lets users tag and document data assets

- **System tables (Public Preview)**: Unity Catalog provides operational data, including audit logs, billable usage, and lineage

Let's understand what the Unity Catalog object model looks like:

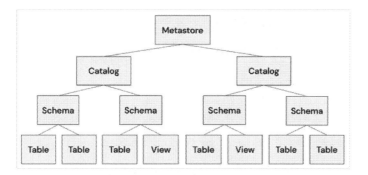

Figure 2.12 – The Unity Catalog object model

The Unity Catalog's hierarchy of primary data objects flows from metastore to table:

- **Metastore**: The top-level container for metadata. Each metastore exposes a three-level namespace (**catalog.schema.table**) that organizes your data.

- **Catalog**: This is the first layer of the object hierarchy and is used to organize your data assets.

- **Schema**: Also known as databases, schemas contain tables and views.

- **Table**: The lowest level in the object hierarchy are tables and views.

As mentioned previously, doing a deep dive into Unity Catalog is a big topic in itself and outside the scope of this book. Unity Catalog offers centralized governance, auditing, and data discovery capabilities for data and AI assets across Databricks workspaces. It provides a secure model based on ANSI SQL, automatic capture of user-level audit logs and data lineage, and a hierarchical data organization system. It also supports a variety of data formats, advanced identity management, specified admin roles for data governance, and is compatible with Databricks Runtime 11.3 LTS or above.

For a more comprehensive understanding of Unity Catalog, go to `https://docs.databricks.com/data-governance/unity-catalog/index.html`.

All the features we've covered so far are standard among all the Databricks persona-specific features.

The following three features, namely experiments, the feature store, and models, are critical for the ML persona.

Let's take a look at them one by one.

Exploring experiments

As the name suggests, experiments are the central location where all the model training pertinent to business problems can be accessed. Users can define their name for the experiment or a default system-generated one and use it to train the different ML model training runs. Experiments in the Databricks UI come from integrating MLflow into the platform. We will dive deeper into MLflow in the coming chapters to understand more details; however, it's important to get a sense of what MLflow is and some of the terminology that is MLflow-specific.

MLflow is an open source platform for managing the end-to-end ML life cycle. Here are the key components of MLflow:

- **Tracking**: This allows you to track experiments to record and compare parameters and results.

- **Models**: This component helps manage and deploy models from various ML libraries to a variety of model serving and inference platforms.

- **Projects**: This allows you to package ML code in a reusable, reproducible form so that you can share it with other data scientists or transfer it to production.

- **Model Registry**: This centralizes a model store for managing models' full life cycle stage transitions: from staging to production, with capabilities for versioning and annotating. Databricks provides a managed version of the Model Registry in Unity Catalog.

- **Model Serving**: This allows you to host MLflow models as REST endpoints.

There are also certain terms specific to MLflow:

- **Run**: A run represents a specific instance of training an ML model. It comprises parameters, metrics, artifacts, and metadata associated with the training process.

- **Experiment**: An experiment serves as a container for organizing and tracking the results of ML experiments. It consists of multiple runs, allowing for easy comparison and analysis of different approaches.

- **Parameter**: A parameter refers to a configurable value that can be adjusted during the training of an ML model. These values influence the behavior and performance of the model.

- **Metric**: A metric is a quantitative measure that's used to evaluate the performance of an ML model. Metrics provide insights into how well the model is performing on specific tasks or datasets.

- **Artifact**: An artifact refers to any output generated during an ML experiment. This can include files, models, images, or other relevant data that captures the results or intermediate stages of the experiment.

- **Project**: A project encompasses the code, data, and configuration necessary to reproduce an ML experiment. It provides a structured and organized approach to managing all the components required for a specific ML workflow.

- **Model**: A model represents a trained ML model that can be utilized to make predictions or perform specific tasks based on the learned patterns and information from the training data.

- **Model registry**: A model registry serves as a centralized repository for storing and managing ML models. It provides versioning, tracking, and collaboration capabilities for different model versions and their associated metadata.

- **Backend store**: The backend store is responsible for storing MLflow entities such as runs, parameters, metrics, and tags. It provides the underlying storage infrastructure for managing experiment data.

- **Artifact store**: The artifact store is responsible for storing artifacts produced during ML experiments. This can include files, models, images, or any other relevant data that's generated throughout the experimentation process.

- **Flavor**: A flavor represents a standardized way of packaging an ML model, allowing it to be easily consumed by specific tools or platforms. Flavors provide flexibility and interoperability when deploying and serving models.

- **UI**: The UI refers to the graphical interface provided by MLflow, allowing users to interact with and visualize experiment results, track runs, and manage models through an intuitive interface.

MLflow also employs additional terms, but the ones mentioned here are some of the most commonly used. For further details, please consult the MLflow documentation: `https://mlflow.org/docs/latest/index.html`.

Databricks AutoML is fully integrated with MLflow, so all the model training and the artifacts that are generated are automatically logged in the MLflow server:

Figure 2.13 – The Experiments tab

End users can also utilize Databricks AutoML to start modeling a solution for their ML problems. Databricks has taken a different approach with its AutoML capability, called **glass box AutoML**.

Databricks AutoML simplifies the workflow for ML practitioners by automatically generating comprehensive notebooks. These notebooks encompass all the necessary code for feature engineering and model training, covering various combinations of ML models and hyperparameters. This feature allows ML practitioners to thoroughly inspect the generated code and gain deeper insights into the process.

Databricks AutoML currently supports classification, regression, and forecasting models. For a list of algorithms that AutoML can use to create models, go to `https://docs.databricks.com/ applications/machine-learning/automl.html#automl-algorithms`:

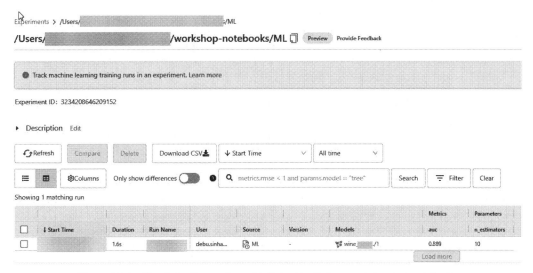

Figure 2.14 – The default experiment is linked to Python notebooks by default

MLflow was developed in-house at Databricks to ease the end-to-end ML life cycle and MLOps. Since the launch of MLflow, it has been widely adopted and supported by the open source community.

Now, let's look at the feature store.

Discovering the feature store

The **feature store** is a relatively new yet stable release in the latest Databricks ML workspace. Many organizations that have mature ML processes in place, such as Uber, Facebook, DoorDash, and many more, have internally implemented their feature stores.

ML life cycle management and workflows are complex. Forbes conducted a survey (`https:// www.forbes.com/sites/gilpress/2016/03/23/data-preparation-most- time-consuming-least-enjoyable-data-science-task-survey-says`) with data scientists and uncovered that managing data is the most expensive and time-consuming operation in their day-to-day work.

Data scientists need to spend a lot of time finding the data, cleaning it, doing EDA, and then performing feature engineering to train their ML models. This is an iterative process. The effort that needs to be put in to make the process repeatable is an enormous challenge. This is where feature stores come in.

Databricks Feature Store is standardized on the open source Delta format, which allows data scientists to govern features similar to those used to govern access to models, notebooks, or jobs in the Databricks environment.

Databricks Feature Store is unique in a couple of ways:

- It uses Delta Lake to store feature tables. This allows end users to read data from any of the supported languages and connectors outside of Databricks. More can be read here: `https://docs.delta.io/latest/delta-intro.html`.

- The integrated Feature Store UI within the Databricks ML workspace provides end-to-end traceability and lineage of how the features were generated and which downstream models use it in a single unified view. We will look at this in more detail in *Chapter 3*.

Databricks Feature Store also integrates seamlessly with MLflow. This allows Databricks Feature Store to utilize all the great features of MLflow's feature pipelines, as well as to generate features and write them out as feature tables in Delta format. The Feature Store has its own generic model packaging format that is compatible with the MLflow Models component, which lets your models know exactly which features were used to train the models. This integration makes it possible to simplify our MLOps pipeline.

A client can call the serving endpoint either in batch mode or online mode, and the model will automatically retrieve the latest features from the Feature Store and provide inference. We will see practical examples of this in the coming chapters.

You can also read more about the current state of Databricks Feature Store here: `https://docs.databricks.com/machine-learning/feature-store/index.html`

Lastly, let's discuss the model registry.

Discovering the model registry

Models is a fully managed and integrated MLflow model registry available to each deployed Databricks ML workspace. The registry has its own set of APIs and a UI to collaborate with data scientists across the organization and fully manage the MLflow model. Data scientists and ML engineers can develop models in any of the supported ML frameworks (`https://mlflow.org/docs/latest/models.html#built-in-model-flavors`) and package them in a generic MLfLow model format:

Figure 2.15 – The Models tab

The model registry provides features to manage the versioning, tagging, and state transitioning between different environments (moving models from staging to production to archive):

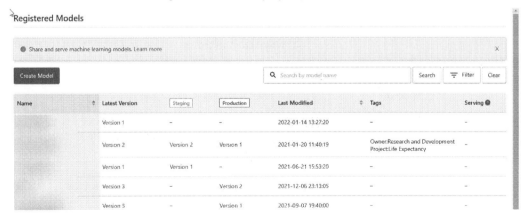

Figure 2.16 – The Registered Models tab

Before we move on, there is another important feature that we need to understand: the **Libraries** feature of Databricks. This feature allows users to utilize third-party or custom code available to Databricks notebooks and jobs running on your cluster.

Libraries

Libraries are fundamental building blocks of any programming ecosystem. They are akin to toolboxes, comprising pre-compiled routines that offer enhanced functionality and assist in optimizing code efficiency. In Databricks, libraries are used to make third-party or custom code available to notebooks and jobs running on clusters. These libraries can be written in various languages, including Python, Java, Scala, and R.

Storing libraries

When it comes to storage, libraries uploaded using the library UI are stored in the **Databricks File System (DBFS)** root. However, all workspace users can modify data and files stored in the DBFS root. If a more secure storage option is desired, you can opt to store libraries in cloud object storage, use library package repositories, or upload libraries to workspace files.

Managing libraries

Library management in Databricks can be handled via three different interfaces: the workspace UI, the **command-line interface (CLI)**, or the Libraries API. Each option caters to different workflows and user preferences, and the choice often depends on individual use cases or project requirements.

Databricks Runtime and libraries

Databricks Runtime comes equipped with many common libraries. To find out which libraries are included in your runtime, you can refer to the **System Environment** subsection of the Databricks Runtime release notes to check your specific runtime version.

Note that Python `atexit` functions aren't invoked by Databricks when your notebook or job finishes processing. If you're utilizing a Python library that registers `atexit` handlers, it's crucial to ensure your code calls the required functions before exiting. Also, the use of Python eggs is being phased out in Databricks Runtime and will eventually be removed; consider using Python wheels or installing packages from PyPI as alternatives.

Library usage modes

Databricks allows three different modes for library installation: cluster-installed, notebook-scoped, and workspace libraries:

- **Cluster libraries**: These libraries are available for use by all notebooks running on a particular cluster.

- **Notebook-scoped libraries**: Available for Python and R, these libraries create an environment scoped to a notebook session and do not affect other notebooks running on the same cluster. They are temporary and need to be reinstalled for each session.

- **Workspace libraries**: These act as local repositories from which you can create cluster-installed libraries. They could be custom code written by your organization or a specific version of an open source library that your organization prefers.

Let's next move on to cover Unity Catalog limitations.

Unity Catalog limitations

There are certain limitations when using libraries with Unity Catalog. For more details, you should refer to the *Cluster libraries* section.

Installation sources for libraries

Cluster libraries can be installed directly from public repositories such as PyPI, Maven, or CRAN. Alternatively, they can be sourced from a cloud object storage location, a workspace library in the DBFS root, or even by uploading library files from your local machine. Libraries installed directly via upload are stored in the DBFS root.

For most of our use cases, we will be using notebook-scoped libraries. You can install notebook-scoped libraries using the `%pip` magic command.

Here are some ways to utilize `%pip` in notebooks to install notebook-scoped libraries:

- **PyPI**: Use `%pip install <package-name>` for notebook-scoped libraries or select PyPI as the source for cluster libraries

- **A private PyPI mirror, such as Nexus or Artifactory**: Use `%pip install <package-name> --index-url <mirror-url>` for notebook-scoped libraries

- **VCS, such as GitHub, with a raw source**: Use `%pip install git+https://github.com/<username>/<repo>.git` for notebook-scoped libraries or select PyPI as the source and specify the repository URL as the package name for cluster libraries

- **DBFS**: Use `%pip install dbfs:/<path-to-package>` for notebook-scoped libraries or select DBFS/S3 as the source for cluster libraries

Now, let's summarize this chapter.

Summary

In this chapter, we got a brief overview of all the components of the Databricks ML workspace. This will enable us to utilize these components in a more hands-on fashion so that we can train ML models and deploy them for various ML problems efficiently in the Databricks environment.

In the next chapter, we will start working on a customer churn prediction problem and register our first feature tables in the Databricks feature store.

Further reading

To learn more about the topics that were covered in this chapter, take a look at the following topics:

- Databricks libraries: `https://docs.databricks.com/libraries/index.html`
- Databricks notebooks: `https://docs.databricks.com/notebooks/index.html`

Part 2: ML Pipeline Components and Implementation

At the end of this section, you will have a good understanding of each of the ML components that are available in the Databricks ML experience and will be comfortable using them in your projects.

This section has the following chapters:

- *Chapter 3, Utilizing the Feature Store*
- *Chapter 4, Understanding MLflow Components on Databricks*
- *Chapter 5, Create a Baseline Model Using Databricks AutoML*

3

Utilizing the Feature Store

In the last chapter, we briefly touched upon what a **feature store** is and how **Databricks Feature Store** is unique in its own way.

This chapter will take a more hands-on approach and utilize Databricks Feature Store to register our first feature table and discuss concepts related to Databricks Feature Store.

We will be covering the following topics:

- Diving into feature stores and the problems they solve
- Discovering feature stores on the Databricks platform
- Registering your first feature table in Databricks Feature Store

Technical requirements

All the code is available on the GitHub repository `https://github.com/PacktPublishing/ Practical-Machine-Learning-on-Databricks` and is self-contained. To execute the notebooks, you can import the code repository directly into your Databricks workspace using **Repos**. We discussed Repos in the second chapter.

Working knowledge of **Delta** format is required. If you are new to Delta format, check out `https:// docs.databricks.com/en/delta/index.html` and `https://docs.databricks. com/en/delta/tutorial.html` before going forward.

Diving into feature stores and the problems they solve

As more teams in the organization start to use AI and ML to solve various business use cases, it becomes necessary to have a centralized, reusable, and easily discoverable feature repository. This repository is called a feature store.

All the curated features are in centralized, governed, access-controlled storage, such as a curated data lake. Different data science teams can be granted access to feature tables based on their needs. Like in enterprise data lakes, we can track data lineage; similarly, we can track the lineage of a feature table logged in Databricks Feature Store. We can also see all the downstream models that are consuming features from a registered feature table.

There are hundreds of data science teams tackling different business questions in large organizations. Each team may have its own domain knowledge and expertise. Performing feature engineering often requires heavy processing. Without a feature store, it becomes difficult for a new group of data scientists to reuse the features created and curated by another data science team.

We can think of feature store workflows as being similar to ETL workflows that cater to a specific type of BI or analytics use case. The workflows that write data to feature store tables cater to a particular feature-engineering process that needs to be performed on the curated dataset in your data lake before training an ML model.

You can schedule and monitor the execution of feature table workflows just like a regular ETL operation.

Feature stores also solve the problem of *skew* between model training and inference code by providing a central repository of features across the organization. The same feature-engineering logic is used during model training and inference.

Let's look at how Feature Store has been built and integrated with the Databricks workspace.

Discovering feature stores on the Databricks platform

Each Databricks workspace has its own feature store. At the time of writing this book, **Databricks Feature Store** only supports the Python API. The latest Python API reference is located at `https://docs.databricks.com/applications/machine-learning/feature-store/python-api.html`.

Databricks Feature Store is fully integrated with **Managed MLFlow** and other Databricks components. This allows models that are deployed by utilizing MLFlow to automatically retrieve the features at the time of training and inference. The exact steps involved in defining a feature table and using it with model training and inference are going to be covered in the following sections.

Let's look at some of the key concepts and terminology associated with Databricks Feature Store.

Feature table

As the name suggests, a feature store stores features generated by data scientists after doing feature engineering for a particular problem.

These features may come from one or more clean and curated tables in the data lake. A feature table in Databricks contains two main components:

- **Metadata**: The metadata tracks the source of the data utilized to create the feature table, which notebooks and scheduled jobs write data into the feature table, and at what frequency. The metadata also tracks downstream ML models utilizing the feature table. This provides lineage.

- **Generated feature data**: In the case of batch and streaming inference, the underlying generated feature DataFrame is written out as a Delta table to an offline feature store. Databricks manages this offline feature store for you. In contrast, the feature table is written out to a supported **relational database management system (RDBMS)** for an **online feature store**. The online feature store is not managed by Databricks and requires some additional steps to set up. There is a link in the *Further reading* section that you can refer to in order to set up an online feature store.

Let's briefly understand the different types of inference patterns and how Databricks Feature Store can be beneficial in each scenario before moving forward:

- **Batch inference**: Batch inference involves making predictions on a large set of data all at once, typically in intervals or scheduled runs. In Databricks, you can set up batch jobs using technologies such as **Apache Spark** to process and predict input data. Batch inference is well suited for scenarios where timely predictions are not critical and you can afford to wait for results. For instance, this could be used in customer segmentation, where predictions are made periodically. This scenario is supported by an offline feature store.

  - Databricks Feature Store enhances batch inference by providing a centralized repository for feature data. Instead of recalculating features for every batch job, Feature Store allows you to store and manage pre-computed features. This reduces computation time, ensuring consistent and accurate features for your models during each batch run.

- **Streaming inference**: Streaming inference involves processing and making predictions on data as it arrives in real time, without waiting for the entire dataset to be collected. Databricks supports streaming data processing using tools such as Apache Spark's **Structured Streaming**. Streaming inference is valuable when you need to respond quickly to changing data, such as in fraud detection where immediate action is crucial. This scenario is supported by an offline feature store.

  - Feature Store plays a key role in streaming scenarios by providing a reliable source of feature data. When new data streams in, Feature Store can supply the necessary features for predictions, ensuring consistent and up-to-date input for your models. This simplifies the streaming pipeline, as feature preparation is decoupled from the real-time inference process.

- **Real-time inference**: Real-time inference takes streaming a step further by delivering instantaneous predictions as soon as new data arrives. This is essential in applications such as recommendation systems, where users expect immediate responses to their actions. This scenario requires an online feature store.

  - For real-time inference, Feature Store ensures that feature data is readily available for quick predictions. Feature Store's integration into the real-time inference pipeline enables low-latency access to features, contributing to swift and accurate predictions. This is crucial in applications demanding rapid decision-making.

Each feature table has a primary key that uniquely defines a row of data. Databricks Feature Store allows defining composite keys as well.

New data can be written into the feature tables using regularly executed ETL pipelines in a batch fashion or a continuous style utilizing the Structured Streaming API (https://docs.databricks.com/spark/latest/structured-streaming/index.html).

The workflow to register a new feature table in Databricks is as follows:

1. Create a database that will store our feature tables.

2. Write feature-engineering logic as a function that returns an Apache Spark DataFrame (https://spark.apache.org/docs/latest/api/python/reference/api/pyspark.sql.DataFrame.html). This DataFrame should also produce a unique primary key for each record in the DataFrame. The primary key can have more than one column as well.

3. Instantiate an object of `FeatureStoreClient` and use `create_table` (supported in DB ML Runtime 10.2 and above) to define a feature table in the feature store. At this point, there is no data stored in the feature table. If we initialize an additional `df` argument with the value of the feature-engineered DataFrame, we can skip *step 4*.

4. Use the `write_table` method to write the feature-engineered dataset into the defined feature table. The `write_table` method provides modes to either completely overwrite the existing feature table or update certain records based on the defined lookup key.

The code example provided in this chapter will go through the aforementioned steps and make them clearer to understand. Before we dive deeper into the code, we need to understand some more concepts related to the feature store.

We will look more at reading from the feature table in the chapter on MLFlow. We will reuse the feature table we created in this chapter to predict bank customer churn.

Offline store

The Databricks offline feature store is backed by Delta tables and is utilized for model training, batch inferencing, and feature discovery.

Delta tables allow users to update feature values based on the primary key in this mode. Utilizing the Delta format also provides additional advantages in the context of ML:

- **Time travel**: With Delta tables, you can access data from any historical point. This is useful when you are debugging inconsistent model performance or probing the impact of data changes on the model. Time travel facilitates a robust audit trail. You can specify `timestampAsOf` to read certain historical data:

```
# Reading data from a Delta table as it appeared at a specific
timestamp
df = spark.read.format("delta").option("timestampAsOf", "2021-
01-01").load("/path/to/delta-table")
```

- **Versioning**: Delta tables also track all data alterations as versions. Each version of the table represents the state of the data and metadata at a particular moment. Delta format tables automatically manage version history for a table to maintain data and metadata consistency. You can access the Delta version history using the `history()` function in the Delta API (`https://docs.delta.io/latest/index.html`):

```
from delta.tables import *
deltaTable = DeltaTable.forPath(spark, write_path)
fullHistoryDF = deltaTable.history()# get the full history of
the table to pick the version
display(fullHistoryDF)
```

To load data from a particular version of the table, we can specify the `versionAsOf` option:

```
## Specifying data version to use for model training
version = 1
df_delta = spark.read.format('delta').option('versionAsOf',
version).load(write_path)
```

This way, you can now train models on different versions of your data and maintain the lineage.

Online store

When using a feature store for real-time inference, the feature table needs to be stored in low-latency storage such as a relational database.

If you must have your features available both in online and offline feature stores, you can use your offline store as a streaming source to update your online store's feature tables.

Training Set

While training an ML model, you may want to combine data from multiple feature tables. Each feature table needs to have a unique ID(s) or primary key(s) that is used at the time of model training and inference to join and retrieve the relevant features from multiple feature tables to the **Training Set** construct.

A training set makes use of an object called `FeatureLookup`, which takes as input the feature table name, feature names that we need to retrieve from the feature table, and a lookup key(s). The lookup key(s) are used to join the features from various feature tables if we define multiple `FeatureLookup` to generate a Training Set.

In the notebook accompanying this chapter, we will go over example code that registers a fraud detection dataset as a feature table in Databricks Feature Store. In *Chapter 5*, *Create a Baseline Model Using Databricks AutoML*, in relation to the AutoML overview, we will take the feature table generated to build a churn prediction model and showcase various components of integrated MLFlow in the Databricks environment.

Model packaging

The `FeatureStoreClient` API (`https://docs.databricks.com/en/dev-tools/api/python/latest/feature-store/client.html`) provides a method called `log_model` that allows ML models to retain the references to the features utilized to train the model. These features reside in Databricks Feature Store as feature tables. The ML model can retrieve the necessary features from the feature tables based on the primary key(s) provided at the time of inference. The feature values are retrieved in the batch and streaming inference mode from the offline store. The retrieved features are combined with any new feature provided during inference before making a prediction. In the real-time inference mode, feature values are retrieved from the online store.

> **Note**
>
> At the time of writing this book, Databricks Feature Store only supports the Python language. You can use your favorite libraries, such as `sklearn` and pandas, to do feature engineering; however, before you write the table out as a feature table, it needs to be converted to a **PySpark** DataFrame. PySpark is a Python wrapper on top of the Spark distributed processing engine (`https://spark.apache.org/docs/latest/api/python/`).

Let's dive into a hands-on example that will walk you through the process of registering your first feature table in Databricks Feature Store.

The dataset we will work with comes from **Kaggle**, and we are going to register this dataset after doing some feature engineering in Databricks Feature Store.

Registering your first feature table in Databricks Feature Store

Before we get started, the code needs to be downloaded from the Git repository accompanying this book (`https://github.com/debu-sinha/Practical_Data_Science_on_Databricks.git`).

We will use the Databricks repository feature to clone the GitHub repo.

To clone the code repository, complete the following steps:

1.   Click on the **Repos** tab and select your username:

Figure 3.1 – A screenshot displaying the Repos tab

Important note

In light of a recent user interface update, the 'Repos' section has been moved and can now be accessed by clicking on the 'Workspaces' icon, as illustrated in the following image.

Despite this change, the workflow outlined in this chapter remains applicable.

2. Right-click and add the repo:

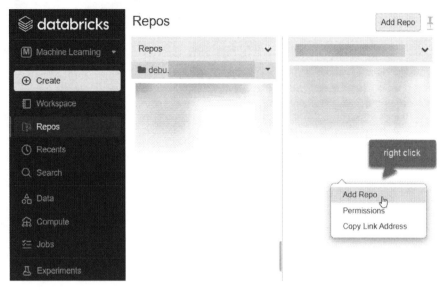

Figure 3.2 – A screenshot displaying how to clone the code for this chapter (step 2)

3. Paste the link into the **Git repo URL** field and click **Create**:

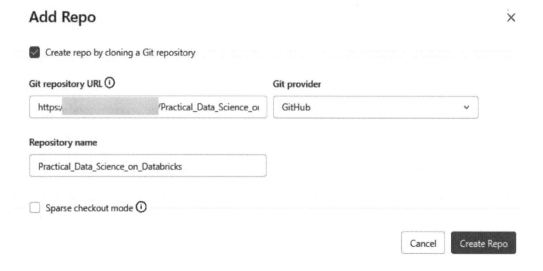

Figure 3.3 – A screenshot displaying how to clone the code for this chapter (step 3)

4. In the cloned repository, click on `Chapter 03` and, within that, the `churn-analysis` notebook:

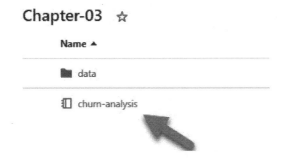

Figure 3.4 – A screenshot displaying how to clone the code for this chapter (step 4)

When you first open the notebook, it will be in the detached stage. If you have not provisioned a cluster, please refer to the *Exploring clusters* section in *Chapter 2*.

You can see the notebook in the following screenshot:

Figure 3.5 – A screenshot displaying the initial state of the notebook

5. After you have a cluster ready to use, you can attach it to the notebook:

Figure 3.6 – A screenshot displaying the dropdown for attaching a notebook to a list of available clusters

All the code has been tested on Databricks ML Runtime 10.4 LTS. I would recommend users have a cluster provisioned with ML Runtime 10.4 LTS or above.

6. Select an option from the drop-down menu:

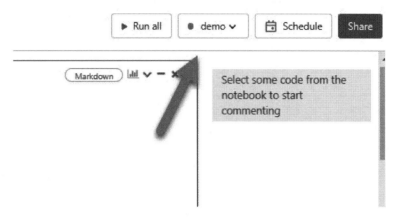

Figure 3.7 – A screenshot displaying the notebook attached to a cluster in the ready state

Now, you are ready to start executing the code in the notebook:

1. The first few cells in the notebook describe the dataset we are working with and how to read it as a Spark DataFrame. We can also import the data as a pandas DataFrame. Databricks has a handy display function that visualizes the data loaded into a pandas or Spark DataFrame:

```
import os
bank_df = spark.read.option("header", True).
option("inferSchema", True).csv(f"file:{os.getcwd()}/data/churn.
csv")
display(bank_df)
```

2. The next block of code goes over the steps to create a feature table. The first step is to define a database that will store the feature tables that we define backed by the Delta tables. We also define a method for performing some basic feature engineering:

```
DATABASE_NAME = "bank_churn_analysis"
# setup database and tmp space that will hold our Feature tables
in Delta format.
spark.sql(f"CREATE DATABASE IF NOT EXISTS {DATABASE_NAME}")
dbutils.fs.mkdirs(f"/tmp/{DATABASE_NAME}")
```

3. The following code block defines a basic function that performs feature engineering on the input Spark DataFrame.

Before going forward, I would like to highlight a powerful library called `pyspark.pandas`. As an ML practitioner, you might be familiar with using the pandas (`https://pandas.pydata.org/docs/#`) library for manipulating data. It has one big drawback in that it's not scalable. All the processing using the pandas API happens on a single machine and if your data cannot fit on a single machine, you will be stuck. This is where Apache Spark can help. Apache Spark is built to handle massive amounts of data as it chunks large amounts of data into individual units and distributes the processing on multiple nodes of a cluster. As the volume of data you want to process increases, you can simply add more nodes to the cluster, and if your data doesn't have any skews, the performance of your data processing pipeline will remain the same.

However, there is a big challenge: many ML practitioners are unfamiliar with the Spark libraries. This is the core reason for developing the `pyspark.pandas` (`https://spark.apache.org/docs/latest/api/python/reference/pyspark.pandas/index.html`) library. This library aims to bridge the gap between the pandas library and Apache Spark.

At the heart of the `pyspark.pandas` library lies its ability to offer a pandas-like API within the realm of Apache Spark. This innovation brings forth the best of both worlds, granting users access to a familiar DataFrame API while harnessing Spark's scalability and performance prowess. For those well versed in pandas, the transition to `pyspark.pandas` is seamless, paving the way for streamlined adoption. However, it's important to keep in mind that not all panda APIs are implemented in the `pyspark.pandas` API, leading to compatibility issues.

If you really have a need to use certain pandas API functionality that is not yet available in `pyspark.pandas`, you can use a method called `toPandas()` (`https://spark.apache.org/docs/latest/api/python/reference/pyspark.sql/api/pyspark.sql.DataFrame.toPandas.html?highlight=topandas`). As a best practice, try to use the PySpark/`pyspark.pandas` API before going for the pandas API. You can read more about best practices at `https://spark.apache.org/docs/latest/api/python/user_guide/pandas_on_spark/best_practices.html?highlight=pandas#use-pandas-api-on-spark-directly-whenever-possible`.

```python
import pyspark.pandas as ps
def compute_features(spark_df):
    # Convert to pyspark.pandas DataFrame # https://spark.
apache.org/docs/3.2.0/api/python/user_guide/pandas_on_spark/
pandas_pyspark.html#pyspark
    ps_df = spark_df.to_pandas_on_spark() #https://spark.apache.
org/docs/3.2.0/api/python/reference/pyspark.pandas/api/pyspark.
pandas.DataFrame.drop.html#pyspark.pandas.DataFrame.drop
    # drop RowNumber & Surname column
    ps_df = ps_df.drop(['RowNumber', 'Surname'], axis=1)
    # OHE (One hot encoding)
    ohe_ps_df = ps.get_dummies(
      ps_df,
```

```
        columns=["Geography", "Gender"],
        dtype="int",
        drop_first=True
    )
    ohe_ps_df.columns = ohe_ps_df.columns.str.replace(r' ', '',
regex=True)
    ohe_ps_df.columns = ohe_ps_df.columns.str.replace(r'(', '-',
regex=True)
    ohe_ps_df.columns = ohe_ps_df.columns.str.replace(r')', '',
regex=True)
    return ohe_ps_df
```

4. The next code block performs feature engineering, utilizing the function defined in the previous section, and displays it:

```
bank_features_df = compute_features(bank_df)
display(bank_features_df)
```

5. Next, we will initialize `FeatureStoreClient`, register the table, and define our feature table structure using the `create_table` function:

```
# Our first step is to instantiate the feature store client
using `FeatureStoreClient()`.
from databricks.feature_store import FeatureStoreClient
fs = FeatureStoreClient()
bank_feature_table = fs.create_table(
  name=f"{DATABASE_NAME}.bank_customer_features", # the name of
the feature table
  primary_keys=["CustomerId"], # primary key that will be used
to perform joins
  schema=bank_features_df.spark.schema(), # the schema of the
Feature table
  description="This customer level table contains one-hot
encoded categorical and scaled numeric features to predict bank
customer churn."
)
```

6. Once we have defined the structure of our feature table, we can populate data in it using the `write_table` function:

```
fs.write_table(df=bank_features_df.to_spark(), name=f"{DATABASE_
NAME}.bank_customer_features", mode="overwrite")
```

Instead of overwriting, you can choose `merge` as an option if you want to update only certain records.

In practice, you can populate the feature table when you call the `create_table` method itself by passing in the source Spark DataFrame as the `feature_df` parameter. This approach can be useful when you have a DataFrame ready to initialize the feature table.

7.   Now we can explore our feature table in the integrated feature store UI. We can see who created the feature table and the data sources that populated the feature table. The feature store UI has a lot of important information about our feature table:

Figure 3.8 – A screenshot displaying details of the feature store

8.   We can examine when a feature table was created, and by whom, through Databricks' user interface. This information is particularly valuable for tracking data provenance and understanding data lineage within the organization. Additionally, the UI displays other pertinent information such as the last time the table was refreshed, giving insights into how up to date the table's data is:

Figure 3.9 – A screenshot displaying details about the owner, primary
key, creation, and last update date of the feature table

Furthermore, the UI provides details about the table's partitions and primary keys. Partitions are crucial for query optimization, as they enable more efficient data retrieval by segregating the table into different subsets based on specific column values. Primary keys, on the other hand, serve as unique identifiers for each row in the table, ensuring data integrity and facilitating quick lookups.

9.   In the production environment, if our feature table is populated regularly through a notebook, we can also visualize historical updates:

Figure 3.10 – A screenshot displaying details about the source of the feature table

10. Lastly, we can also view the data types of every feature in the feature table:

▼ Features (13)

Feature	Data Type
Age	INTEGER
Balance	DOUBLE
CreditScore	INTEGER
CustomerId	INTEGER
EstimatedSalary	DOUBLE
Exited	INTEGER
Gender_Male	LONG
Geography_Germany	LONG
Geography_Spain	LONG
HasCrCard	INTEGER

Figure 3.11 – A screenshot displaying details about the various
columns of the feature table and the data types

The notebook is heavily documented and will walk you through all the steps required to get raw data, from importing to Databricks to writing out your first feature table.

To understand the current limitations and other administrative options available with Databricks Feature Store, refer to `https://docs.databricks.com/en/machine-learning/feature-store/troubleshooting-and-limitations.html`.

Summary

In this chapter, we got a deeper understanding of feature stores, the problems they solve, and a detailed look into the feature store implementation within the Databricks environment. We also went through an exercise to register our first feature table. This will enable us to utilize the feature table to create our first ML model as we discussed in the MLFlow chapter.

Next, we will cover MLFlow in detail.

Further reading

- Databricks, *Repos for Git Integration*: `https://docs.databricks.com/repos.html#repos-for-git-integration`
- You can read more about the supported RDBMS here: `https://docs.databricks.com/applications/machine-learning/feature-store/concepts.html#online-store`
- You can read more on how the feature tables are joined together with the training DataFrame here: `https://docs.databricks.com/applications/machine-learning/feature-store/feature-tables.html#create-a-trainingset-when-lookup-keys-do-not-match-the-primary-keys`
- Apache Spark, *Apache Arrow in PySpark*: `https://spark.apache.org/docs/latest/api/python/user_guide/sql/arrow_pandas.html`
- Databricks, *Convert PySpark DataFrames to and from pandas DataFrames*: (`https://docs.databricks.com/spark/latest/spark-sql/spark-pandas.html#convert-pyspark-dataframes-to-and-from-pandas-dataframes`)

4

Understanding MLflow Components on Databricks

In the previous chapter, we learned about Feature Store, what problem it solves, and how Databricks provides the built-in Feature Store as part of the Databricks **machine learning** (**ML**) workspace, which we can use to register our feature tables.

In this chapter, we will look into managing our model training, tracking, and experimentation. In a software engineer's world, code development and productionization have established best practices; however, such best practices are not generally adopted in the ML engineering/data science world. While working with many Databricks customers, I observed that each data science team has its own way of managing its projects. This is where MLflow comes in.

MLflow is an umbrella project developed at Databricks, by Databricks engineers, to bring a standardized ML life cycle management tool to the Databricks platform. It is now an open source project with more than 500,000 daily downloads on average as of September 2023 and has broad industry and community support. MLflow provides features to manage the end-to-end ML project life cycle. Some of the features are only available on Databricks.

In this chapter, we will cover the following topics:

- Overview of MLflow
- MLflow Tracking
- MLflow Projects
- MLflow Models
- MLflow Model Registry
- Example code showing how to track ML model training in Databricks

These components play an essential role in standardizing and streamlining your ML project's life cycle. When we use MLflow with Databricks, some MLflow features are more helpful than others. We'll point out the most useful ones as we go through this chapter.

Technical requirements

All the code is available in this book's GitHub repository `https://github.com/PacktPublishing/Practical-Machine-Learning-on-Databricks` and is self-contained. To execute the notebooks, you can import the code repository directly into your Databricks workspace using repos. We discussed repos in our previous chapters.

This chapter also assumes that you have a preliminary understanding of what user-defined functions are in Apache Spark. You can read more about them here: `https://docs.databricks.com/en/udf/index.html`.

Overview of MLflow

The ML life cycle is complex. It starts with ingesting raw data into the data/Delta lake in raw format from various batch and streaming sources. The data engineers create data pipelines using tools such as Apache Spark with Python, R, SQL, or Scala to process a large amount of data in a scalable, performant, and cost-effective manner.

The data scientists then utilize the various curated datasets in the data lake to generate feature tables to train their ML models. The data scientists prefer programming languages such as Python and R for feature engineering and libraries such as scikit-learn, pandas, NumPy, PyTorch, or any other popular ML or deep learning libraries for training and tuning ML models.

Once the models have been trained, they need to be deployed in production either as a **representational state transfer (REST) application programming interface (API)** for real-time inference, or a **user-defined function (UDF)** for batch and stream inference on Apache Spark. We also need to apply monitoring and governance around the deployed model. In case of drift in model performance or data, we may need to retrain and redeploy the model.

This process is iterative and brings a lot of development challenges to organizations looking to start working on ML projects:

- A zoo of software tools needs to be managed to provide a stable working environment for the data scientists. A large number of libraries need to be manually installed and configured.

- Tracking and reproducing the results of ML experiments is also a challenge.

- Managing the services and governance around productionizing models is difficult.

- Scaling the training of the models with the increase in the amount of data is a challenge.

MLflow, with its components, provides a solution to each of these challenges. In the Databricks environment, MLflow is integrated with workspace components such as notebooks, Feature Store, and AutoML. This integration provides a seamless experience for data scientists and ML engineers who are looking to get productive without getting into the operational overhead of managing the installation of MLflow on their own:

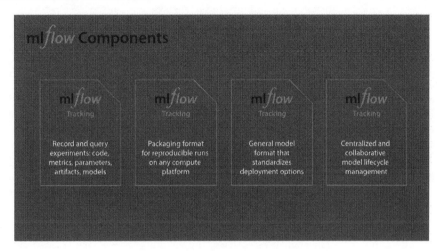

Figure 4.1 – The various components of MLflow

Four software components make up MLflow:

- **MLflow Tracking**
- **MLflow Projects**
- **MLflow Models**
- **MLflow Model Registry**

In Databricks, all these components except MLflow Projects are integrated, fully managed, and provided as services as part of the Databricks workspace. As our primary focus is on MLflow features seamlessly integrated with Databricks, we won't delve extensively into MLflow Projects. Rest assured, this won't impact your ML project workflow when using Databricks. The Databricks ML workspace also offers high availability, automated updates, and access controls for all the integrated MLflow components.

Let's take a look at each of these components in detail.

MLflow Tracking

MLflow Tracking allows you to track the training of your ML models. It also improves the observability of the model-training process. The MLflow Tracking feature allows you to log the generated metrics, artifacts, and the model itself as part of the model training process. MLflow Tracking also keeps track of model lineage in the Databricks environment. In Databricks, we can see the exact version of the notebook responsible for generating the model listed as the source.

MLflow also provides **automatic logging (autolog)** capabilities that automatically log many metrics, parameters, and artifacts while performing model training. We can also add our own set of metrics and artifacts to the log.

Using MLflow Tracking, we can chronologically track model training. Certain terms are specific to MLflow Tracking. Let's take a look at them:

- **Experiments**: Training and tuning the ML model for a business problem is an experiment. By default, each Python notebook in Databricks has an experiment with the same name. This is called a notebook-scoped experiment. You can easily change and set the experiment's name using the MLflow API. Defining an experiment like this will create a workspace-scoped MLflow experiment that will now be visible in your workspace. Customizing the names of MLflow experiments offers valuable benefits in ML workflows – for example, it enhances organizational clarity by helping you categorize and differentiate experiments, acting as a form of documentation that aids communication and collaboration. Custom names facilitate version control and the tracking of experiment evolution, which is particularly useful for comparing performance or revisiting past configurations. Additionally, they simplify the process of accessing specific experiments through MLflow's user interface or programmatic queries, ultimately contributing to more efficient and effective ML project management. We will be using a custom experiment name for our example code.

- **Runs**: We can have multiple models training with different hyperparameters logged under each experiment. Each of the unique combinations of ML model training logged under an experiment is called a run. The accompanying MLflow Tracking UI allows us to compare and contrast the different runs and get the best model.

- **Metrics**: Each run will have critical offline metrics that we want to log while training our models. Unlike online metrics, which are calculated in real time as a model interacts with live data and users, offline metrics are computed retrospectively using a fixed dataset that was collected before the model's deployment. These metrics are crucial during the model development and testing phases to gauge how well a model generalizes to unseen data and to guide model refinement. Common examples of offline metrics include accuracy, precision, recall, F1-score, **mean squared error (MSE)**, and **area under the receiver operating characteristic curve (AUC-ROC)**, among others. They provide insights into a model's performance and can inform decisions regarding hyperparameter tuning, feature engineering, and model selection to improve overall predictive accuracy and effectiveness.

- **Artifacts**: MLflow artifacts play a pivotal role in MLflow's experiment tracking system by facilitating the storage and versioning of supplementary files and data linked to ML experiments. These versatile artifacts can encompass a variety of resources, including ML model files, datasets, configuration files, data visualizations (for example, plots), documentation (for example, READMEs and Jupyter notebooks), custom scripts, and even reports summarizing experiment findings. Crucially, artifacts are versioned alongside experiment runs, ensuring precise tracking of changes over time. They support remote storage solutions and are programmatically accessible via MLflow's API. This comprehensive approach enhances reproducibility, organization, and collaboration in ML projects, making it possible to recreate experiments accurately and access all relevant resources.

- **Parameters**: Parameters are user-defined configuration settings or hyperparameters associated with ML experiment runs. They play a vital role in tracking, comparing, and reproducing experiments by recording the specific configuration settings used in each run. This allows for easy visualization and analysis of how parameter values impact experiment outcomes, making it simpler to identify optimal configurations and manage experiments effectively.

- **Tags**: Tags are user-defined or automatically generated metadata labels that can be attached to ML experiment runs. They serve to provide context, categorization, and organization for runs, aiding in searching for, filtering, and analyzing experiments. Tags help document and distinguish different runs, making it easier to understand and manage ML projects, and they can be used for custom workflow integration or automation.

Next, we will understand one of the key components of MLflow called MLflow Models.

MLflow Models

MLflow Models is a standard packaging format for ML models. It provides a standardized abstraction on top of the ML model created by the data scientists. Each MLflow model is essentially a directory containing an `MLmodel` file in the directory's root that can define multiple flavors that the model can be viewed in.

Flavors represent a fundamental concept that empowers MLflow Models by providing a standardized approach for deployment tools to comprehend and interact with ML models. This innovation eliminates the need for each deployment tool to integrate with every ML library individually. MLflow introduces several "standard" flavors, universally supported by its built-in deployment tools. For instance, the "Python function" flavor outlines how to execute the model as a Python function. However, the versatility of flavors extends beyond these standards. Libraries have the flexibility to define and employ their own flavors. As an example, MLflow's `mlflow.sklearn` library allows you to load models as scikit-learn pipeline objects, suitable for use in scikit-learn-aware code, or as generic Python functions, catering to tools requiring a model application, such as the MLflow deployments tool with the `-t sagemaker` option for deploying models on Amazon SageMaker. So, flavors serve as a bridge between ML libraries and deployment tools, enhancing interoperability and ease of use.

You can register an MLflow model from a run in an experiment using the `mlflow.<model-flavor>.log_model` method. This method serializes the underlying ML model in a specific format and persists it in the underlying storage.

Check out the official documentation for a complete list of ML libraries supported by MLflow Models: `https://www.mlflow.org/docs/latest/models.html#built-in-model-flavors`. If you have some existing models that were developed using any Python ML library, MLflow provides a method to create custom models via the `mlflow.pyfunc` module.

Additional files are logged, such as `conda.yaml` and `requirements.txt`, that contain the library dependencies for recreating the runtime environment when needed.

The ML model YAML file contains the following attributes:

- `time_created`: The date and time in UTC ISO 8601 format describing when the model was created.

- `flavors`: This defines how downstream applications can use this model.

- `run_id`: This represents the unique identifier for the MLflow run; this model was logged under B.

- `signature`: The model signature in JSON format. This signature defines the expected format of input and output data for an ML model. It is automatically inferred from datasets representing valid input and output examples, such as the training dataset and model predictions.

- `input_example`: This is for if we provide sample records as input while training the model.

The MLflow Models API provides a method called `mlflow.evaluate()` that automatically evaluates our trained model on an evaluation dataset and logs the necessary metrics, such as accuracy, R2, and SHAP feature importance based on what kind of problem we are trying to solve. You can also create custom metrics and provide them as input to `mlflow.evaluate(custom_metrics=[<your custom metric>])` as a parameter. Links have been provided in the *Further reading* section if you want to learn more about it.

MLflow Models also provide APIs to deploy the packaged ML models as a REST endpoint for real-time inference, as a Python function that can be used to perform batch and stream inference, or as a Docker container that can then be deployed to Kubernetes, Azure ML, or AWS SageMaker. The MLflow API provides convenient methods such as `mlflow.models.build_docker` to build and configure a Docker image. You can read more about the various methods that are available here: "`https://www.mlflow.org/docs/latest/python_api/mlflow.models.html?highlight=docker#mlflow.models.build_docker`". We will look into the various available deployment options as part of Databricks integrated with MLflow in *Chapter 7, Model Deployment Approaches*.

Now, let's look at the next feature on the list: MLflow Model Registry.

MLflow Model Registry

MLflow Model Registry is a tool that collaboratively manages the life cycle of all the MLflow Models in a centralized manner across an organization. In Databricks, the integrated Model Registry provides granular access control over who can transition models from one stage to another.

MLflow Model Registry allows multiple versions of the models in a particular stage. It enables the transition of the best-suited model between staging, prod, and archived states either programmatically or by a human-in-the-loop deployment model. Choosing one strategy over another for model deployment will depend on the use case and how comfortable teams are in automating the entire process of managing ML model promotion and testing process. We will take a deeper look into this in *Chapter 6, Model Versioning and Webhooks*.

Model Registry also logs model descriptions, lineage, and promotion activity from one stage to another, providing full traceability.

We will look into the Model Registry feature more in detail in *Chapter 6, Model Versioning and Webhooks*.

The following figure summarizes the interaction between various MLflow components:

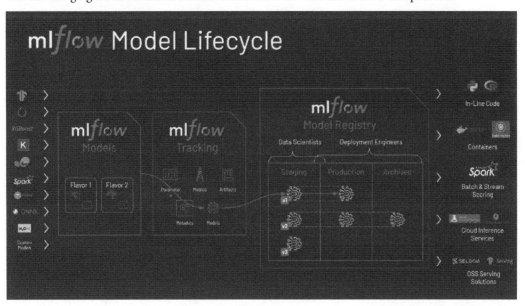

Figure 4.2 – How the various MLflow components interact with each other

You have the flexibility to choose your preferred Python ML libraries for model training within MLflow, while the MLflow Tracking server diligently logs metrics, tags, and artifacts, and then packages your model into the MLflow Models format. Once you've honed a candidate model ready for integration into Model Registry, it's a straightforward process to register it there. Model Registry not only furnishes APIs but also offers governance mechanisms for smooth model transitioning between stages. Additionally,

MLflow Model Registry introduces webhooks, which enable automated notifications to be triggered by specific user actions; we'll delve into this further in *Chapter 6, Model Versioning and Webhooks*. In the end, downstream applications can harness APIs to fetch the latest models from the registry and deploy them in various flavors, including Python functions, Docker containers, or other supported deployment options that accommodate batch, streaming, and real-time use cases.

You have the freedom to independently manage your ML project life cycle by employing the features we've discussed thus far, even without utilizing Databricks Feature Store. However, utilizing Feature Store in ML projects offers numerous advantages, including centralized data management for streamlined access and consistency, feature reusability across projects, version control for reproducibility, data quality checks, collaborative teamwork, scalability to handle growing data complexity, real-time feature serving, model monitoring integration, regulatory compliance support, and significant time and cost savings. In essence, Feature Store enhances the efficiency and effectiveness of ML workflows by providing a structured and efficient approach to data management and feature handling.

Let's look at an end-to-end code example that goes through the entire flow of training an ML model in the Databricks environment and utilizes all the features of integrated MLflow.

Example code showing how to track ML model training in Databricks

Before proceeding, it's important to ensure that you've already cloned the code repository that accompanies this book, as outlined in *Chapter 3*. Additionally, please verify that you have executed the associated notebook for *Chapter 3*. These preparatory steps are essential to fully engage with the content and exercises presented here:

1. Go to Chapter 04 and click on the `mlflow-without-featurestore` notebook:

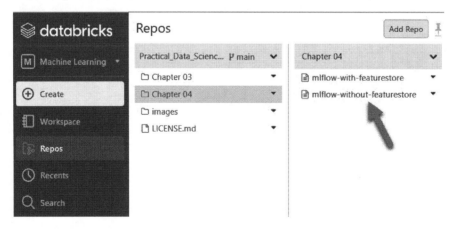

Figure 4.3 – The code that accompanies this chapter

Make sure you have a cluster up and running and that the cluster is attached to this notebook, as you did with the notebook from *Chapter 3, Utilizing the Feature Store.*

2. Cmd 3 demonstrates the use of notebook-scoped libraries. These can be installed using the %pip magic command. As best practice, keep the %pip command as one of the topmost cells in your notebook as it restarts the Python interpreter. We are just upgrading the version of the scikit-learn library here:

```
%pip install -U scikit-learn
```

3. In Cmd 5 and Cmd 6, we are just defining some constant values we will be using to track our ML model training. Change the USER_EMAIL value to the email you've used to log into the Databricks workspace. In this notebook, we are not going to use the Feature Store API; however, every feature table is stored as a Delta table, which can be read as a regular hive table:

```
from databricks.feature_store import FeatureStoreClient
from databricks.feature_store import FeatureLookup
import typing
from sklearn import metrics
from sklearn.ensemble import RandomForestClassifier
from sklearn.model_selection import train_test_split
import mlflow
import pandas as pd
# Name of experiment where we will track all the different model
training runs.
EXPERIMENT_NAME = "Bank_Customer_Churn_Analysis"
# Name of the model
MODEL_NAME = "random_forest_classifier"
# This is the name for the entry in model registry
MODEL_REGISTRY_NAME = "Bank_Customer_Churn"
# The email you use to authenticate in the Databricks workspace
USER_EMAIL = "<your email>"
# Location where the MLflow experiment will be listed in user
workspace
EXPERIMENT_NAME = f"/Users/{USER_EMAIL}/{EXPERIMENT_NAME}"
# we have all the features backed into a Delta table so we will
read directly
FEATURE_TABLE = "bank_churn_analysis.bank_customer_features"
```

4. To use Mlflow, we had to import the mlflow package. mlflow.setExperiment(...) creates a named experiment to track all the MLflow runs that we will execute in this notebook. After executing this code, you should be able to see a new type of entity listed in your workspace directory where EXPERIMENT_NAME points to. As mentioned earlier, this creates a workspace-scoped experiment:

```
# set experiment name
mlflow.set_experiment(EXPERIMENT_NAME)
```

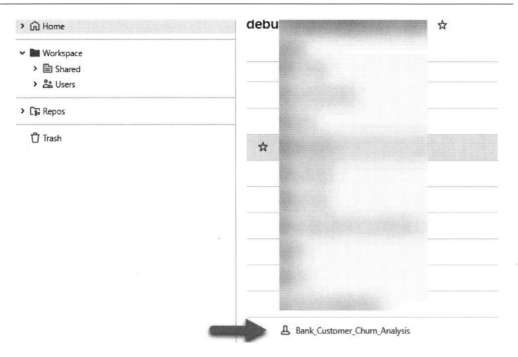

Figure 4.4 – The new experiment that was created in the workspace

5. Calling `mlflow.start_run()` starts a run under the listed experiment. The rest of the code simply trains a scikit learn model. With just a few lines of code, we are now using the features of MLflow Tracking:

```
with mlflow.start_run():
  TEST_SIZE = 0.20

  # Now we will read the data directly from the feature table
  training_df = spark.table(FEATURE_TABLE)

  # convert the dataset to pandas so that we can fit sklearn
RandomForestClassifier on it
  train_df = training_df.toPandas()

  # The train_df represents the input dataframe that has all
the feature columns along with the new raw input in the form of
training_df.
  X = train_df.drop(['Exited'], axis=1)
  y = train_df['Exited']
  X_train, X_test, y_train, y_test = train_test_split(X, y,
test_size=TEST_SIZE, random_state=54, stratify=y)
```

```
  # here we will are not doing any hyperparameter tuning
however, in future we will see how to perform hyperparameter
tuning in scalable manner on Databricks.
  model = RandomForestClassifier(n_estimators=100).fit(X_train,
y_train)
  signature = mlflow.models.signature.infer_signature(X_train,
model.predict(X_train))

  predictions = model.predict(X_test)
  fpr, tpr, _ = metrics.roc_curve(y_test, predictions, pos_
label=1)
  auc = metrics.auc(fpr, tpr)
  accuracy = metrics.accuracy_score(y_test, predictions)

  # get the calculated feature importances.
  importances = dict(zip(model.feature_names_in_, model.feature_
importances_))
  # log artifact
  mlflow.log_dict(importances, "feature_importances.json")
  # log metrics
  mlflow.log_metric("auc", auc)
  mlflow.log_metric("accuracy", accuracy)
  # log parameters
  mlflow.log_param("split_size", TEST_SIZE)
  mlflow.log_params(model.get_params())
  # set tag
  mlflow.set_tag(MODEL_NAME, "mlflow demo")
  # log the model itself in mlflow tracking server
  mlflow.sklearn.log_model(model, MODEL_NAME,
signature=signature, input_example=X_train.iloc[:4, :])
```

6. The following code utilizes the MLflow Tracking server to log artifacts and hyperparameter values while setting tag to the sklearn model that is being logged to the MLflow Tracking server:

```
  mlflow.log_dict(importances, "feature_importances.json")
  # log metrics
  mlflow.log_metric("auc", auc)
  mlflow.log_metric("accuracy", accuracy)
  # log parameters
  mlflow.log_param("split_size", TEST_SIZE)
  mlflow.log_params(model.get_params())
  # set tag
  mlflow.set_tag(MODEL_NAME, "mlflow demo")
  # log the model itself in mlflow tracking server
  mlflow.sklearn.log_model(model, MODEL_NAME,
signature=signature, input_example=X_train.iloc[:4, :])
```

Once we've finished executing the code in this cell, we will be able to see the run and all its artifacts, parameters, and hyperparameters listed under the experiment:

Figure 4.5 – The runs listed under the experiments

7. You can check the details of each run in the Tracking UI by clicking the shortcut icon:

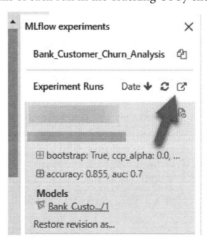

Figure 4.6 – The shortcut for accessing the integrated MLflow Tracking UI

The Tracking UI displays information about each run in a lot more detail. Along with the serialized model, you can access logged artifacts, metrics, hyperparameters, the model signature, or the sample input that your model expects as input if you logged them during the run. At the top, you can see the path to the experiment under which this run is being tracked. Each run is uniquely identified with an ID that is also visible at the top. The tracking server provides lineage and links this model run back to the exact version of the notebook that was used to execute this run:

Figure 4.7 – The details of the run in the Tracking UI

8. Clicking on the experiment path at the top will take you to the experiment view where, if you have executed more than one run, you can select and compare various runs to get the best model or compare the best combinations of the hyperparameters:

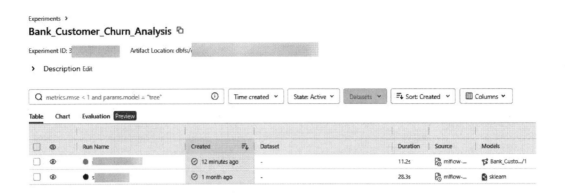

Figure 4.8 – All the runs associated with our experiment

Now, let's summarize this chapter.

Summary

In this chapter, we covered the various components of MLflow and how they work together to make the end-to-end ML project life cycle easy to manage. We learned about MLflow Tracking, Projects, Models, and Model Registry.

This chapter covered some key components of MLFlow and their purpose. Understanding these concepts is essential in effectively managing end-to-end ML projects in the Databricks environment.

In the next chapter, we will look at the AutoML capabilities of Databricks in detail and how we can utilize them to create our baseline models for ML projects.

5
Create a Baseline Model Using Databricks AutoML

In the last chapter, we understood **MLflow** and all its components. After running the notebook from *Chapter 4, Understanding MLflow Components on Databricks*, you might have recognized how easy it actually is to start tracking your ML model training in Databricks using the integrated MLflow tracking server. In this chapter, we will cover another new and unique feature of **Databricks** called **AutoML**.

Databricks AutoML, like all the other features that are part of the Databricks workspace, is fully integrated with MLflow features and the Feature Store.

Databricks AutoML, at the time of writing of this book, supports **classification**, **regression**, and **forecasting** use cases using traditional ML algorithms and not deep learning. You can see a list of supported algorithms in the second section of the chapter.

You can use AutoML with a table registered in Databricks' Hive metastore, feature tables, or even upload a new file using the import data functionality in Databricks. You can read more about it by clicking the link in the *Further reading* section.

In this chapter, we will cover the following topics:

- Understanding the need for AutoML
- Understanding AutoML in Databricks
- Running AutoML on our churn prediction dataset
- Current limitations

Let's go through the technical requirements for this chapter.

Technical requirements

To go through the chapter, we'll need the following requirements:

- we'll need the execution of the notebooks pertaining to *Chapter 3*, which involves the ingestion of raw data from a CSV file into a Delta table and the subsequent registration of a new feature table, to have already been completed.

Understanding the need for AutoML

If you have never worked with any AutoML framework before, you might be wondering what AutoML is and when and how it can be useful.

AutoML simplifies the machine learning model development process by automating various tasks. It automatically generates baseline models tailored to your specific datasets and even offers preconfigured notebooks to kickstart your projects. This is particularly appealing to data scientists of all levels of expertise because it saves valuable time in the initial stages of model development. Instead of manually crafting models from scratch, AutoML provides a quick and efficient way to obtain baseline models, making it a valuable tool for both beginners and experienced data scientists alike.

AutoML makes machine learning not only accessible to citizen data scientists and business subject matter experts. AutoML, while undoubtedly a powerful tool, also grapples with significant limitations. One notable challenge is its inherent black-box nature, which makes it difficult, and at times impossible, to decipher which hyperparameters and algorithms are most effective for a particular problem. This opacity presents a substantial obstacle when it comes to achieving model explainability.

Furthermore, many AutoML tools available in the market fall short of supporting essential components in the machine learning life cycle, including the critical step of operationalizing models for production use. This deficiency can hinder the seamless integration of machine learning solutions into real-world applications.

It's important to note that AutoML doesn't replace the role of a data scientist. While it streamlines certain aspects of model development, the expertise and insights of a skilled data scientist remain indispensable in ensuring the success of machine learning projects.

This is where Databricks AutoML actually provides one of its biggest benefits. Let's take a deeper look into AutoML in Databricks and discover how you can use it in your model development journey.

Understanding AutoML in Databricks

Databricks AutoML uses a glass-box approach to AutoML. When you use Databricks AutoML either through the UI or through the supported Python API, it logs every combination of model and hyperparameter (trial) as an MLflow run and generates Python notebooks with source code corresponding to each model trial. The results of all these model trials are logged into the MLflow tracking server. Each of the trials can be compared and reproduced. Since you have access to the source code, the data scientists can easily rerun a trial after modifying the code. We will look at this in more detail when we go over the example.

Databricks AutoML also prepares the dataset for training and then performs model training and hyperparameter tuning on the Databricks cluster. One important thing to keep in mind here is that Databricks AutoML spreads hyperparameter tuning trials across the cluster. A trial is a unique configuration of hyperparameters associated with the model. All the training datasets should fit in a single executor, as Databricks AutoML will automatically sample your dataset if you have a large dataset.

At the time of writing the book, Databricks AutoML supports the following algorithms:

ML problems	Supported algorithms
Classification	<ul><li>Scikit-learn models:<ul><li>Decision trees</li><li>Random forests</li><li>Logistic regression</li></ul></li><li>XGBoost</li><li>LightGBM</li></ul>
Regression	<ul><li>Scikit-learn models:<ul><li>Linear regression with stochastic gradient descent</li><li>Decision trees</li><li>Random forests</li></ul></li><li>XGBoost</li><li>LightGBM</li></ul>
Forecasting	<ul><li>Prophet</li><li>Auto ARIMA</li></ul>

Table 5.1 – Algorithms that Databricks AutoML supports

Let's understand some of the key capabilities provided by Databricks AutoML in more detail.

Sampling large datasets

Sampling is done based on the estimated memory required to load and train models on the training dataset. Until ML Runtime 10.5, the data sampling does not depend on the VM type or the amount of memory the executor is running on. In ML Runtime 11.0 and later versions, the sampling mechanism will increase sampling fraction and size if a node is compute-optimized with more significant memory.

By default, in Databricks, each executor is configured to execute the same number of trials as there are available CPU cores. Additionally, the executor's available memory is evenly distributed among these trials. However, you have the flexibility to modify this behavior by adjusting the `spark.task.cpus` configuration parameter.

The default setting for `spark.task.cpus` is 1, which means that each executor will run as many trials in parallel as it has CPU cores. If you change this value to match the number of available CPU cores on the executor, it will result in a different behavior. In this case, only one trial will be executed on the executor at a time, but that trial will have access to the full memory capacity of the executor. This setting can be useful if you want to provide additional resources to each of your trials. This will also increase the size of the sampled dataset. AutoML utilizes the PySparks `sampleBy` method (`https://spark.apache.org/docs/latest/api/python/reference/api/pyspark.sql.DataFrameStatFunctions.sampleBy.html`) for performing stratified sampling for classification problems.

For regression problems, AutoML utilizes the `sample` method (`https://spark.apache.org/docs/latest/api/python/reference/api/pyspark.sql.DataFrame.sample.html`) when sampling is needed.

Sampling is not applicable for forecasting problems.

Imbalance data detection

In Databricks Runtime 11.2 ML and newer versions, when AutoML detects an imbalanced dataset for a classification use case, it takes steps to mitigate the imbalance within the training dataset. This is accomplished through a combination of downsampling the major class(es) and introducing class weights. It's important to note that this balancing process is applied exclusively to the training dataset and doesn't affect the test and validation datasets. This approach guarantees that the model's performance is evaluated based on the original dataset with its true class distribution.

To address an imbalanced training dataset, AutoML assigns class weights that are inversely proportional to the extent of downsampling applied to a specific class. To illustrate, let's consider a training dataset with 100 samples, where 95 belong to `Class A` and 5 belong to `Class B`. AutoML reduces this imbalance by downsampling `Class A` to 70 samples, effectively reducing it by a ratio of 70:95, or approximately 0.736. Meanwhile, the number of samples in `Class B` remains at five. To ensure that the final model is properly calibrated and maintains the same probability distribution as the input data, AutoML adjusts the class weight for `Class A` by the inverse of this ratio, which is approximately

1:0.736, or 1.358. The weight for `Class B` remains at one. These class weights are then used during the model training process as a parameter to ensure that samples from each class receive appropriate weighting, contributing to a balanced and accurate model.

Splitting data into train/validation/test sets

In Databricks Runtime 10.1 ML and later versions, you have the option to designate a time column when performing data splits for classification and regression tasks. When you specify this time column, the dataset is divided into training, validation, and test sets based on chronological order. The data points from the earliest time period are allocated to the training set, followed by the next earliest for validation. The most recent data points are reserved for the test set.

In Databricks Runtime 10.1 ML, the time column must be of either the timestamp or integer data type. However, starting from Databricks Runtime 10.2 ML, you also have the flexibility to choose a string column for this purpose. This enhancement offers greater versatility in time-based data splitting for improved model training and evaluation.

Enhancing semantic type detection

Semantic type detection is a powerful feature, introduced in Databricks Runtime versions 9.1 LTS ML and beyond, designed to augment AutoML by providing intelligent insights into the data types present within each column. *It is essential to note that semantic type detection does not apply to forecasting problems or columns where custom imputation methods have been specified.*

AutoML conducts a thorough analysis of columns to ascertain whether their semantic type differs from the data type specified in the table schema (either Spark or pandas). Once discrepancies are identified, AutoML takes specific actions based on the detected semantic type. However, it's important to keep in mind that these detections may not always be 100% accurate. The following are the key adjustments AutoML can make:

- **String and integer columns with date or timestamp data**: These are intelligently recognized as timestamp types, allowing for more precise handling of temporal information
- **String columns representing numeric data**: When applicable, these columns are converted into numeric types, ensuring that mathematical operations can be performed seamlessly

Starting from Databricks Runtime 10.1 ML, AutoML extends its capabilities to encompass the following:

- **Numeric columns containing categorical IDs**: These are identified as categorical features, aiding in more accurate modeling when dealing with categorical data
- **String columns containing English text**: Such columns are identified as text features, enhancing the understanding of textual data within the dataset

In Databricks Runtime version 10.1 ML and beyond, users gain the ability to manually set semantic types through Python annotations. The following code snippet illustrates the syntax for this manual annotation process:

```
metadata_dict = df.schema["<column-name>"].metadata
metadata_dict["spark.contentAnnotation.semanticType"] = "<semantic-
type>"
df = df.withMetadata("<column-name>", metadata_dict)
```

The available semantic types that you can assign manually are as follows:

- **Categorical**: Appropriate for columns containing values such as IDs
- **Numeric**: Ideal for columns containing numeric values
- **DateTime**: Suitable for columns with timestamp values
- **Text**: Reserved for string columns containing English text

To disable semantic type detection for a specific column, you can use the special keyword annotation native.

Shapley value (SHAP) for model explainability

Shapley values (**SHAP**) are a technique grounded in game theory used to estimate the significance of each feature in a machine learning model's predictions. AutoML regression and classification notebooks come with built-in code to compute these values using the SHAP package. However, because calculating SHAP is highly memory-intensive, they are not enabled by default.

To activate and compute SHAP in an AutoML notebook, you need to navigate to the **Feature importance** tab, set shap_enabled to True, and then rerun the notebook. It's worth noting that SHAP plots won't be generated in version 11.1 and earlier versions of MLR if the dataset includes a DateTime column.

Feature Store integration

In Databricks Runtime version 11.3 LTS ML and subsequent releases, feature tables from the Feature Store can be utilized to enhance the base dataset for classification and regression tasks. As of version 12.2 LTS ML, this capability extends to augmenting the input dataset for a comprehensive set of AutoML challenges, including classification, regression, and forecasting.

There are certain limitations associated with the current state of AutoML. Only the following data types in your dataset are supported:

- Numeric (ByteType, ShortType, IntegerType, LongType, FloatType, and DoubleType)
- Boolean
- String (categorical or English text)

- Timestamps (*TimestampType* and *DateType*)
- `ArrayType[Numeric]` (Databricks Runtime 10.4 LTS ML and later versions)
- `DecimalType` (Databricks Runtime 11.3 LTS ML and later versions)

You also need to ensure that the source dataset has all unique column names. If you utilize AutoML for time series forecasting and want Auto ARIMA, ensure that the interval between any two points in the time-series input dataset is the same. AutoML will automatically fill the missing timesteps with the previous value by default.

Let's take a look at an example use case for AutoML.

Running AutoML on our churn prediction dataset

Let's take a look at how to use Databricks AutoML with our bank customer churn prediction dataset.

If you executed the notebooks from *Chapter 3*, *Utilizing the Feature Store*, you will have raw data available as a Delta table in your Hive metastore. It has the name `raw_data`. In the *Chapter 3* code, we read a CSV file from our Git repository with raw data, wrote that as a Delta table, and registered it in our integrated metastore. Take a look at `cmd 15` in your notebook. In your environment, the dataset can be coming from another data pipeline or uploaded directly to the Databricks workspace using the *Upload file* functionality.

To view the tables, you need to have your cluster up and running.

Figure 5.1 – The location of the raw dataset

Let's create our first Databricks AutoML experiment.

> **Important note**
>
> Make sure that before following the next steps, you have a cluster up and running that has the following configuration:
>
> Single-node or multi-node
>
> Access mode as a single user
>
> The Databricks runtime version is set to 13.3 LTS ML or higher
>
> *Worker Type/Driver Type* is any VM type with at least four cores
>
> *No additional libraries should be installed on the cluster other than those pre-installed in Databricks Runtime for machine learning. AutoML is not compatible with clusters operating in shared access mode.*

1. On the left tab, click on **Experiments**.

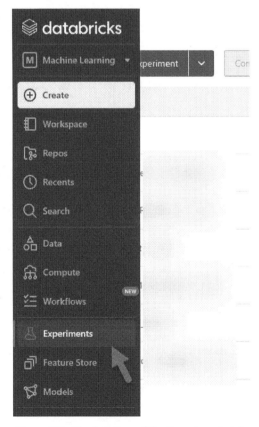

Figure 5.2 – The location of the Experiments tab

2. On the top of this page, click on **Create AutoML Experiment**. This will bring you to the AutoML configuration page.

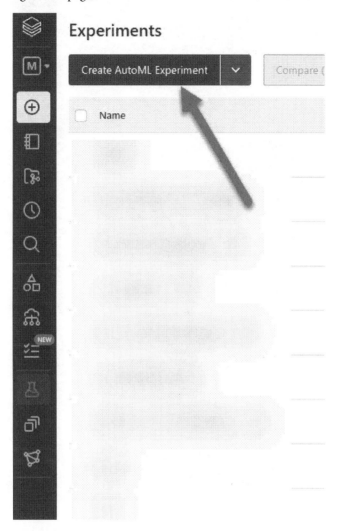

Figure 5.3 – How to create a new AutoML experiment (1)

3. As an alternative, you can click on **New** and then select **AutoML Experiment**.

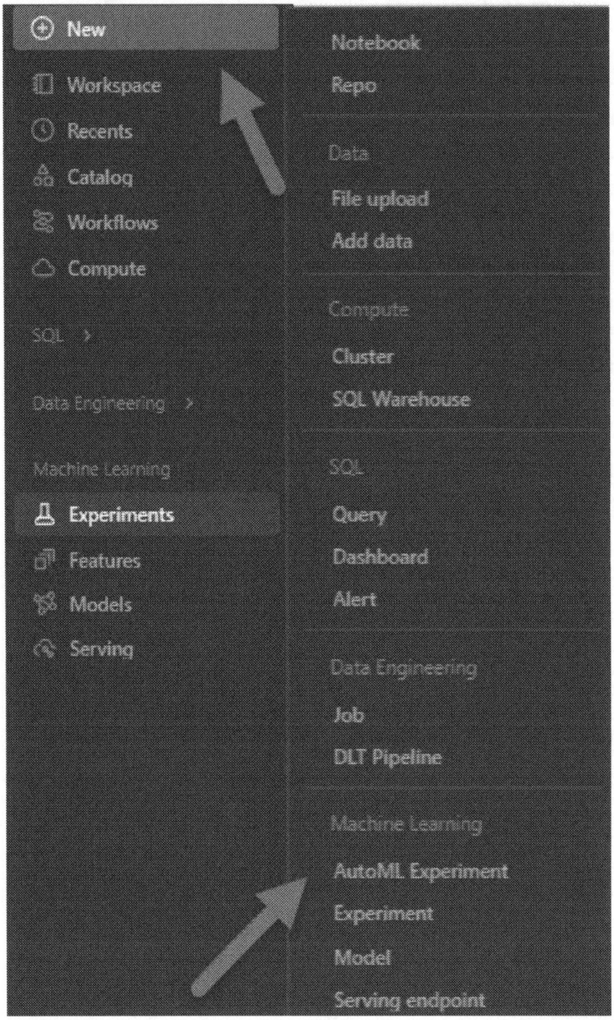

Figure 5.4 – An alternative way to create an AutoML experiment

4. To get started, you need to enter the following basic information:

- **For the purpose of this cluster**: This is what cluster configuration you want the AutoML to run on. You can reuse the same cluster we created for *Chapter 3, Utilizing the Feature Store*, and *Chapter 4, Understanding MLflow Components on Databricks*.

- **ML problem type**: Regression, classification, or forecasting.
- **Dataset**: The dataset containing all the features and label/target column.

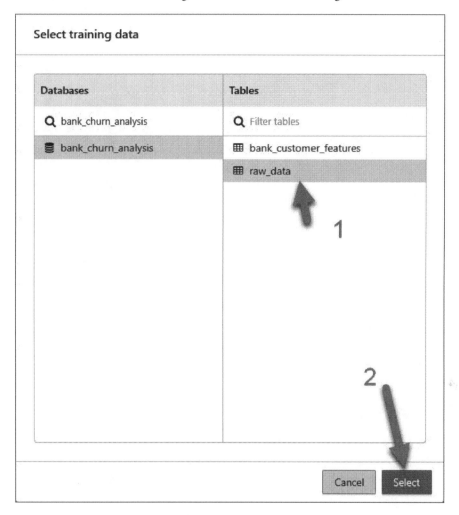

Figure 5.5 – How to create a new AutoML experiment (2)

- **Prediction target**: This is specific to the classification problem at hand. Once you select your dataset for running AutoML, this will auto-populate with all the columns and you can select your target column.

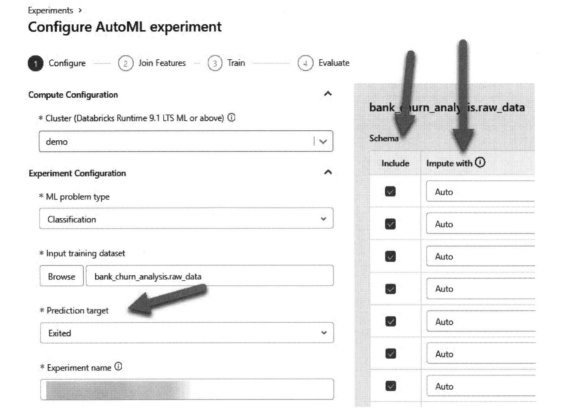

Figure 5.6 – Showing how to create a new AutoML experiment (3)

- **Experiment name**: This is the name that is used to track all your trials.

- Optionally, you can also select what features from your selected table need to be included when running the trials. In our case, RowNumber, CustomerId, and Surname don't add any value to our analysis, so we will remove them from selection.

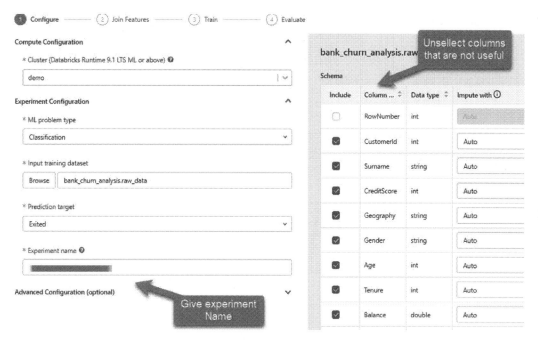

Figure 5.7 – How to create a new AutoML experiment (4)

Optionally, you can also select how you would want to handle missing values in your dataset.

In versions 10.4 LTS ML and higher of Databricks Runtime, you can define the approach for handling null values. Within the UI, you can select your desired imputation technique via the **Impute with** drop-down menu located within the table **Schema** section.

It's worth noting that AutoML automatically chooses an appropriate imputation strategy based on both the data type and the content of the column in question.

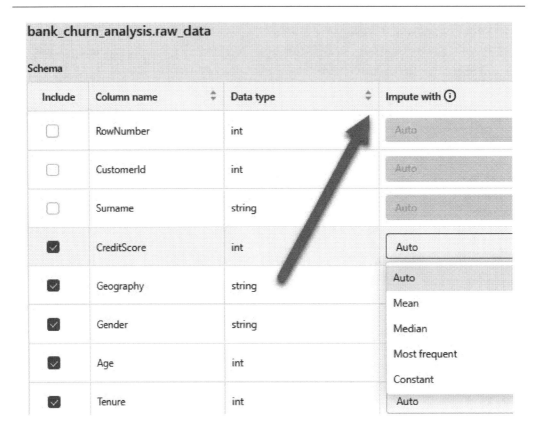

Figure 5.8 – How to create a new AutoML experiment (5)

That's it! Those are the only five things you need to do to start using glassbox AutoML with Databricks.

There are some advanced configurations as well, such as what metrics you want to optimize when selecting the best-performing model or what supported training framework you want to include to run trials on:

- The evaluation metric serves as the primary scoring metric for runs.

- Starting from Databricks Runtime 10.3 ML, it's possible to exclude certain training frameworks. By default, AutoML uses frameworks listed under its algorithms.

- Stopping conditions are customizable. The defaults are as follows:

  - Stop after 120 minutes for forecasting experiments.

  - For classification and regression experiments in Databricks Runtime 10.5 ML and earlier versions, stop after 60 minutes or after 200 trials—whichever comes first. Starting from Databricks Runtime 11.0 ML, the number of trials is not a stopping condition.

- From Databricks Runtime 10.1 ML, AutoML incorporates early stopping for classification and regression if the validation metric ceases to improve.

- Also starting from Databricks Runtime 10.1 ML, you can select a time column for chronological data splitting in classification and regression tasks.

- You can specify a DBFS location for saving the training dataset in the **Data directory** field. If left blank, the dataset is saved as an MLflow artifact.

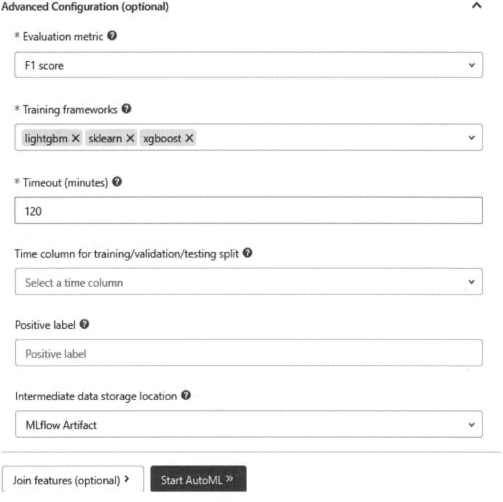

Figure 5.9 – How to create a new AutoML experiment (6)

To enhance the richness of your dataset, you can seamlessly integrate an existing feature table. Simply scroll to the bottom of the page and click on the **Join Features** option. This will grant you access to a configuration panel where you can precisely specify which feature tables you want to merge with your existing dataset and establish the key or keys that will underpin this merging process, effectively linking the datasets.

However, it's important to note that for the sake of this example, we will not be incorporating the *Feature store* table into the *merge* operation. This approach empowers you to bolster your dataset with additional information from selected feature tables, elevating its utility for analytical or machine-learning endeavors while omitting the Feature Store table from this particular exercise.

Now we simply need to hit **start AutoML**:

- Our AutoML experiment is now executing and is the current state visible in the UI. As AutoML progresses, it produces the following three artifacts:

  - It generates a detailed data exploration notebook with source code to outline any skews or concerns, such as missing data or zeros. It uses the `pandas.profiling` package automatically to do this. You can view this notebook by clicking **View data exploration notebook**.

Figure 5.10 – How to access the auto-generated exploratory data analysis notebook

The data exploration notebook also displays the correlation between the different features:

Correlations

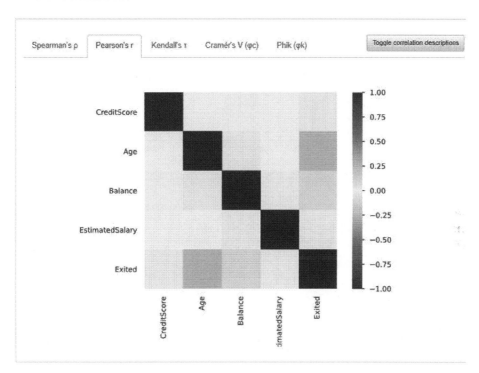

Figure 5.11 – Correlation graphs generated by the exploratory data analysis notebook

- You can see the experiment trials containing source code for every run being performed on our dataset. The source code is listed under your workspace under your user directory in a folder called `databricks_automl`.

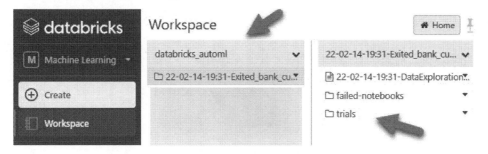

Figure 5.12 – The location of various notebooks with code relating to each trial

- The notebook with the best model is also generated from AutoML after all the trials have finished execution. This notebook walks you through all the steps performed to feature engineer and train the ML model. The trial is logged automatically in the tracking server. The notebook also contains code for feature transformation.

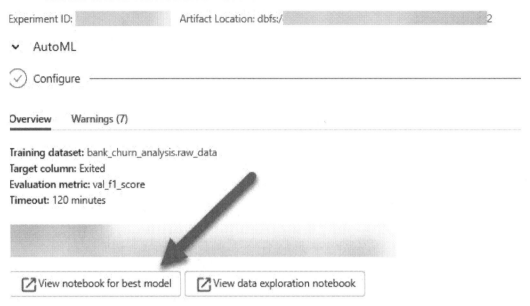

Figure 5.13 – The location of the notebook that logs the best model identified by AutoMl

It also utilizes SHAP (https://pypi.org/project/shap/) to log feature importance.

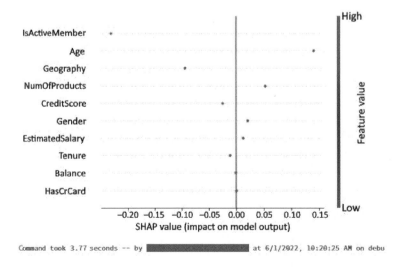

Figure 5.14 – A sample SHAP value graph auto-generated as part of the best model notebook

This notebook also explains how you can finally utilize the trained model using the various deployment options, which we will discuss later in *Chapter 6, Model Versioning and Webhooks*.

- You can compare the various trials through the UI.

- You can also utilize the Python API to kick off AutoML for classification, forecasting, or regression. Using the Python API, you can also retrieve the best model programmatically from the AutoML experiment and use it for inference.

This is an example code for kicking off classification:

```
databricks.automl.classify(
    dataset: Union[pyspark.DataFrame, pandas.DataFrame],
    *,
    target_col: str,
    data_dir: Optional[str] = None,
    exclude_columns: Optional[List[str]] = None,          # <DBR>
10.3 ML and above
    exclude_frameworks: Optional[List[str]] = None,       # <DBR>
10.3 ML and above
    experiment_dir: Optional[str] = None,                 # <DBR>
10.4 LTS ML and above
    imputers: Optional[Dict[str, Union[str, Dict[str, Any]]]] =
None, # <DBR> 10.4 LTS ML and above
    max_trials: Optional[int] = None,                     #
deprecated in <DBR> 10.3 ML
    primary_metric: str = "f1",
    time_col: Optional[str] = None,
    timeout_minutes: Optional[int] = None,
) -> AutoMLSummary
```

You can read more about the various parameters at `https://docs.databricks.com/applications/machine-learning/automl.html#classification-and-regression`.

Summary

In this chapter, we covered the importance of AutoML and how it can help data scientists get started and become productive with the problem at hand. We then covered the Databricks AutoML glassbox approach, which makes it easy to interpret model results and automatically capture lineage. We also learned how Databricks AutoML is integrated with the MLflow tracking server within the Databricks workspace.

In the next chapters, we will go over managing your ML model's life cycle using the MLflow model registry and Webhooks in more detail.

Further reading

Here are some other useful links:

- Databricks, *What is AutoML?*: (`https://docs.databricks.com/applications/machine-learning/automl.html#databricks-automl`)

- Databricks, *Import data*: (`https://docs.databricks.com/data/data.html#import-data-1`)

Part 3: ML Governance and Deployment

You will learn how to utilize the MLFlow model registry to manage model versioning and transition to production from various stages and use webhooks to set up alerts and monitoring.

This section has the following chapters:

6

Model Versioning and Webhooks

In the previous chapter, we delved deep into the capabilities of **Databricks AutoML**, exploring its various components in detail. We gained a comprehensive understanding of how data science practitioners can harness the power of transparent "glass box" AutoML to kickstart their machine learning solutions seamlessly, especially when tackling complex business challenges.

Furthermore, we put AutoML into action by automating the selection of a candidate model for our **Bank Customer Churn** prediction classification problem. To facilitate this process, we seamlessly integrated the robust MLflow features into our workflow. This integration allowed us to meticulously track every aspect of our model's training, providing us with invaluable insights into its performance and enabling us to make data-driven decisions. Our journey also took us to the MLflow tracking server, where we logged and monitored the entire training process, ensuring that our Bank Customer Churn prediction project was executed with precision and efficiency.

In this chapter, we will look into the next steps on how we can take a model from the **MLflow tracking server** and utilize the integrated **MLflow Model Registry** to manage the model life cycle.

We will cover the following topics:

- Understanding the need for the Model Registry
- Registering your candidate model to the Model Registry and managing access
- Managing the ML model life cycle using the Model Registry
- Diving into the **Webhooks** support in the Model Registry

Technical requirements

Let's go through the technical requirements for this chapter:

- All the previous notebooks, already executed as described

- A Slack workspace where you have webhooks enabled for a channel (`https://api.slack.com/messaging/webhooks`)

Understanding the need for the Model Registry

In traditional software engineering, the concept of a central code repository is well established and mature. However, in the realm of data science, the idea of a centralized model repository is still evolving. While it's not accurate to say that no central repository for models exists – there are indeed other tools and platforms that offer similar functionalities – the challenges in model management are unique and often more complex.

This is where Databricks' integrated MLflow Model Registry shines, particularly in fostering collaboration among data science teams.

Key features of the Model Registry include the following:

- **Centralized discovery**: The Model Registry serves as a centralized hub where models from various data science teams are registered. Each registered model has a lineage that traces back to the original run and the notebook version in which the model was trained, making it easier for teams to collaborate.

- **Life cycle management**: Databricks provides both UI and API options for managing the life cycle of your models, streamlining the process of promoting a model from one stage to another.

- **Automated testing and deployment**: The Model Registry allows you to deploy different versions of a model to various stages. You can also attach notes and perform tests on these models in an automated fashion, ensuring that only the most robust models make it to production.

- **Access control**: Robust permissioning features govern who can access, modify, or deploy a registered model, thereby ensuring that only authorized individuals can interact with your models.

Now, let's take a look at how you can register a model in the Model Registry.

Registering your candidate model to the Model Registry and managing access

You can either use the UI to register a candidate model to the integrated Model Registry or use the MLflow Model Registry API.

Let's take a look at the UI option first:

1. We will first navigate to the MLflow experiment created by our AutoML execution. We can navigate here by clicking on the **Experiments** tab in the left navigation bar:

Figure 6.1 – How to access the Experiments page

2. Next, we select our experiment from the list:

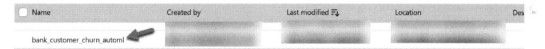

Figure 6.2 – The experiment listed in the integrated MLflow tracking server created by AutoML

3. Now we have access to all the runs that were executed as part of our AutoML execution. Here, we can sort the runs in the UI to get the best F1 score:

Figure 6.3 – Various models and runs associated with the AutoML experiment sorted by F1 score

4. Next, we select the model that is listed as the first option in the list. In my case, this is the `sklearn` model based on LightGBM:

Figure 6.4 – How to look at and access the logged model for the best run

5. Now we will end up at the MLflow **Run** page for this specific model. This page must be looking familiar to you as, when you scroll down, you will see the artifacts, metrics, and hyperparameters all logged automatically as part of our run (we covered this in previous chapters):

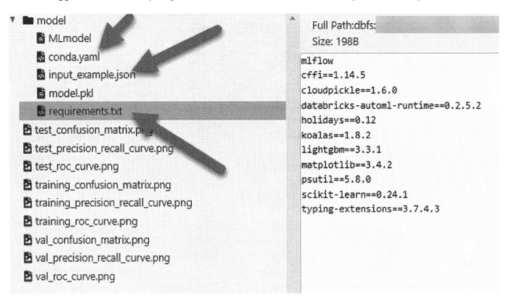

Figure 6.5 – The different artifacts automatically logged by AutoML for each experiment run

On the right side, you will see a button with the caption **Register Model**:

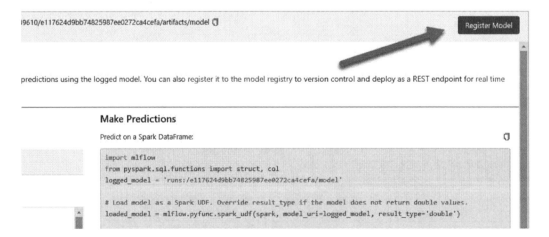

Figure 6.6 – How to register a candidate model to the Model Registry 1

6. If you are using the MLflow Model Registry for the first time, you can select **Create New Model** and give it a sensible name. In my case, I am giving it the name Churn Prediction Bank. Then, hit **Register**:

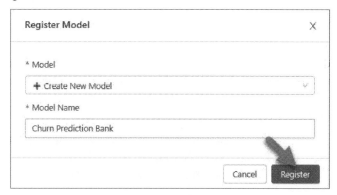

Figure 6.7 – How to register a candidate model to the Model Registry 2

At this point, your model is registered in the Model Registry and should be visible if you access the **Models** page.

7. You can access the **Models** page by clicking on the **Models** icon in the left-hand navigation tab:

Figure 6.8 – How to access the Model Registry

8.   Simply select the **Churn Prediction Bank** model from the list:

Figure 6.9 – The registered candidate model in the Model Registry

A couple of things to observe here are as follows:

- The latest version says **Version 1**. This is because we created a new model entry in the registry. If we select an existing model from the dropdown in *Step 9*, then the version will say **Version 2** and so on.

- Upon clicking on **Version 1**, you will be taken to the details page of this version of the model and see that **Source Run** is listed as **lightgbm**, which is the same run that generated our best model. Also, the input and output schemas are inherited from the model signature in the source run automatically.

You can also set tags and add a description for your model in the UI:

Figure 6.10 – The details of the registered version of the candidate model in the Model Registry

By default, the stage is set to **None**. You can manage permissioning around who has permission to request transitioning your model from one stage to another using the built-in access controls.

9.   You can set permissions at the user or group level by clicking on the **Permissions** tab on the page we interacted with in *Step 8*

Figure 6.11 – How to add governance around model access 1

By default, the workspace admins and the original creator of the model have the **Can Manage** permission:

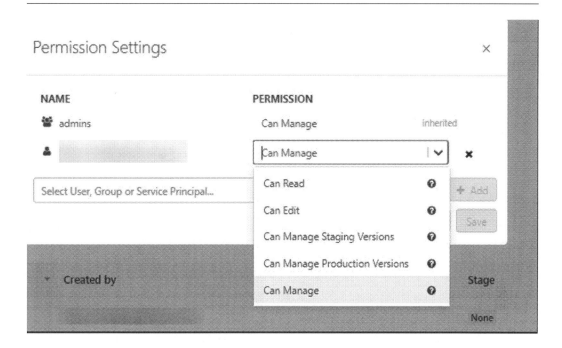

Figure 6.12 – How to add governance around model access 2

You can also specify giving access or control over the model's life cycle by stage. In Databricks MLflow's Model Registry, each model version can be classified into one of three distinct life cycle stages: **Staging**, **Production**, or **Archived**. Notably, it is possible to have multiple model versions coexist within the same life cycle stage. This is particularly beneficial for scenarios such as A/B testing where parallel evaluation of different model versions is essential. However, this feature could present a challenge for organizations in managing and differentiating between multiple models at the same life cycle stage.

To resolve this issue, MLflow offers a tagging mechanism. Tags can be applied to model versions to offer additional metadata, making it easier to identify, filter, and manage models within the same stage. If there are multiple model versions in the same stage, then by default, the most recent version of the model is loaded. However, it's crucial to specify which model version you intend to load, particularly when multiple versions exist within the same stage. In *Chapter 7, Model Deployment Approaches*, we will delve deeper into various methods for deploying these staged models effectively. The user interface allows you to modify the stage of a model version, as illustrated in the following image.

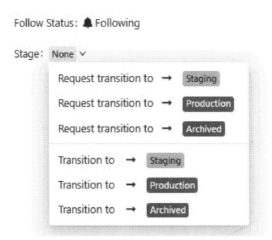

Figure 6.13 – Various options for model stage transition

10. Click on **Request transition to**, then **Staging**. This action will send a notification to the owner of the model that we have requested it to be reviewed and requested its transition to staging. In our case, we will get this notification as we own the model ourselves. We can also add comments to our model transition request:

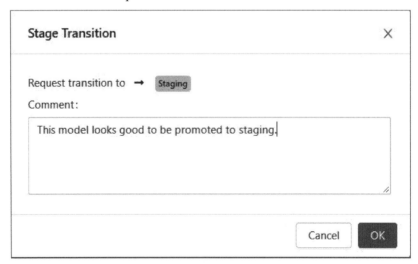

Figure 6.14 – Transitioning a model to staging

11. As the owner of the model, we can then read all the comments on the model and have the option to approve, reject, or cancel the request. On clicking **Approve**, our model is now transitioned into the **Staging** stage:

Figure 6.15 – The documentation history and the ability to approve a model transition request

All the aforementioned actions through the UI can be performed using the MLflow Python API when you want to create automated workflows for model training and deployments.

Let's now look at how you can programmatically register the model into the integrated Model Registry and then transition to staging. Go to the notebook associated with Chapter 06 and open it in the Databricks workspace.

In the third code cell, we programmatically retrieve the most recently modified experiment. The goal is to extract the best-performing model from this experiment based on our chosen evaluation metrics:

```
import mlflow
# Initialize the Mlflow client
client = mlflow.tracking.MlflowClient()
# Fetch all available experiments
```

```
experiments = client.search_experiments()
# Sort the experiments by their last update time in descending order
sorted_experiments = sorted(experiments, key=lambda x: x.last_update_
time, reverse=True)
# Retrieve the most recently updated experiment
latest_experiment = sorted_experiments[0]
# Output the name of the latest experiment
print(f"The most recently updated experiment is named '{latest_
experiment.name}'.")
# Note: If you're specifically looking for the experiment related to
AutoML for base model creation,
# ensure that 'latest_experiment' corresponds to that experiment.
```

In the fifth cell, we first initialize some parameters such as our existing username, experiment_name, which is the experiment's name that's associated with our AutoML, and the registry_model_name, which will be the model's name in the Model Registry. In the earlier section, we already registered our candidate models using the UI in the registry under the name **Bank Customer Churn**. We will use the same model name here. We will also use the MlflowClient library imported from the mlflow.tracking package to access the best model based on **F1 score** by retrieving the run_id associated with the best model run from our MLflow tracking server:

```
# Initialize the Databricks utilities to programmatically fetch the
username
username = dbutils.notebook.entry_point.getDbutils().notebook().
getContext().userName().get()
# Retrieve the name of the latest experiment; assumed to have been set
in earlier steps
experiment_name = latest_experiment.name
# Define the model name for the registry, specific to our use-case of
Churn Prediction for a Bank
registry_model_name = "Churn Prediction Bank"
# Fetch the experiment details using its name
experiment_details = client.get_experiment_by_name(experiment_name)
# Search for runs within the experiment and sort them by validation F1
score in descending order
sorted_runs = mlflow.search_runs(experiment_details.experiment_id).
sort_values("metrics.val_f1_score", ascending=False)
# Get the run ID of the best model based on the highest validation F1
score
best_run_id = sorted_runs.loc[0, "run_id"]
best_run_id
# Note: The variable `best_run_id` now contains the run ID of the best
model in the specified experiment
```

To register the model associated with the best model training run, we need to provide the model URI (the path to the model in our tracking server) as input to the MLflow registry `register_model` API. The other parameter we need to pass is the model's name under which we want the new version of the model retrieved from the model tracking server to register. Since, for the sake of simplicity, we are keeping the name the same as the model name we defined in the UI, the new model will be registered as **version 2** in the Model Registry:

```
# Initialize the model's URI using the best run ID obtained from
previous steps
model_uri = f"runs:/{best_run_id}/model"
# Register the model in Mlflow's model registry under the specified
name
try:
    model_details = mlflow.register_model(model_uri=model_uri,
name=registry_model_name)
    print(f"Successfully registered model '{registry_model_name}' with
URI '{model_uri}'.")
except mlflow.exceptions.MlflowException as e:
    print(f"Failed to register model '{registry_model_name}':
{str(e)}")
model_details
```

You can also use the `MLflowClient` object to update the description or set tags related to a model in the registry. In `Command 9` of the notebook, we demonstrate how you can use the `MLflowClient` object to call the `update_registered_model` and `update_model_version` methods:

```
# Update the metadata of an already registered model
try:
    client.update_registered_model(
        name=model_details.name,
        description="This model predicts whether a bank customer will
churn or not."
    )
    print(f"Successfully updated the description for the registered
model '{model_details.name}'.")
except mlflow.exceptions.MlflowException as e:
    print(f"Failed to update the registered model '{model_details.
name}': {str(e)}")
# Update the metadata for a specific version of the model
try:
    client.update_model_version(
        name=model_details.name,
        version=model_details.version,
        description="This is a scikit-learn based model."
    )
    print(f"Successfully updated the description for version {model_
details.version} of the model '{model_details.name}'.")
```

```
except mlflow.exceptions.MlflowException as e:
    print(f"Failed to update version {model_details.version} of the
model '{model_details.name}': {str(e)}")
```

In Command 11 of the notebook, we demonstrate how you can use the transition_model_stage method using the MLflowClient object to transition the latest model version to the Staging stage. You can also archive the earlier model as we transition the new model to Staging:

```
# Transition the model version to the 'Staging' stage in the model
registry
try:
    client.transition_model_version_stage(
        name=model_details.name,
        version=model_details.version,
        stage="Staging",
        archive_existing_versions=True  # Archives any existing
versions in the 'Staging' stage
    )
    print(f"Successfully transitioned version {model_details.version}
of the model '{model_details.name}' to 'Staging'.")
except mlflow.exceptions.MlflowException as e:
    print(f"Failed to transition version {model_details.version} of
the model '{model_details.name}' to 'Staging': {str(e)}")
```

Let's now explore how to leverage the webhook events provided by the MLflow Model Registry to automate notifications. This will alert us whenever specific events related to models registered in the MLflow registry occur.

Diving into the webhooks support in the Model Registry

A webhook allows users to create custom callbacks to enable communication between web applications. Webhooks allow a system to push data into another system automatically when some event occurs.

As an example, this could apply if you want to automatically trigger a notification on Slack when you detect a new transition request for a model in MLflow, or if you want to trigger a new model build when there is a new code commit in your version control branch.

MLflow webhooks provide capabilities for end users to automatically listen to any events related to the Model Registry and trigger actions. The webhooks can be integrated with messaging systems such as Slack to send notifications or trigger CI/CD pipelines for automatically testing and deploying ML models.

You can use webhooks using the Python client or Databricks REST API.

There are two different types of webhooks that are supported by the MLflow Model Registry based on the target:

- **Webhooks with HTTP endpoints**: These are used when we want to send trigger events to an HTTP endpoint such as Slack.

- **Webhooks for Databricks Jobs**: These are specifically used for sending trigger events to Databricks Jobs. This type of webhook is particularly useful for initiating automated tests on models that have been newly promoted to staging or production environments as part of your CI/CD process.

The following figure summarizes the workflow involving registering a model to the MLflow Model Registry, and how you can utilize MLflow webhooks to kick off Slack notifications and Databricks jobs to apply tags/comments or automate tests on the newly deployed model:

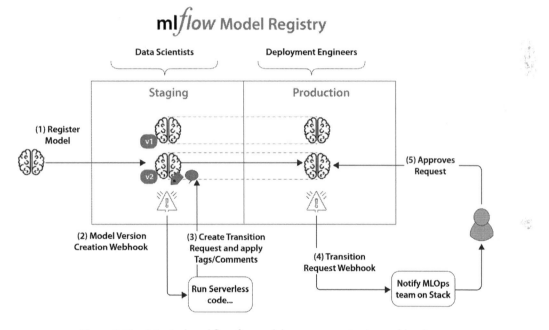

Figure 6.16 – A typical workflow for model management using webhooks

> **Note**
> Courtesy of Databricks

Once a model stage transition request is filed, the HTTP webhook can be used to notify the user/group of users who can review the request and *approve* it.

You can also set webhooks for a specific model or for all the models that are registered in a particular registry.

You can read about the various supported webhook events at `https://docs.databricks.com/en/mlflow/model-registry-webhooks.html#webhook-events`.

In the code example provided with this chapter, we are specifically using the following two events:

- `MODEL_VERSION_CREATED`: A new model version was created for the associated model

- `TRANSITION_REQUEST_CREATED`: A user requested a model version's stage to be transitioned

To demonstrate how you can establish automated alerting for model transitions via Slack, you must first secure a Slack webhook URL. The following steps guide you through the creation of a Slack app and subsequently allow you to set up an incoming webhook. For an exhaustive guide on this subject, please refer to the official Slack API documentation on webhooks at `https://api.slack.com/messaging/webhooks`.

If you're actively running the code from the `Chapter 06` notebook, ensure that you have your Slack webhook URL at hand before proceeding to execute `Command 16`.

> **Note**
>
> One thing to remember here is that the REST endpoints we are going to hit for creating a new registry webhook, deleting webhooks, listing webhooks, and more are only available on Databricks and not on the open source MLflow. You can read more about the Databricks REST API specification for MLflow at `https://docs.databricks.com/dev-tools/api/latest/mlflow.html#operation/get-registered-model`.

Let's proceed with our review of the notebook located in the `Chapter 06` folder. We'll now delve into the details of utilizing webhooks to automatically send notifications to a Slack channel when specific events occur within the model registry concerning your registered model

1. In `Command 15`, we specified a code block that provides utility functions to interact with MLflow's REST API. It initializes an MLflow client and fetches host and token credentials for authentication. The `mlflow_call_endpoint` function is designed to make HTTP calls to a specified MLflow API endpoint using either `GET` or other HTTP methods. It accepts an API endpoint, an HTTP method, and an optional JSON payload as arguments, and returns a JSON response as a dictionary. The script also handles exceptions, printing an error message if the API call fails:

```
from mlflow.utils.rest_utils import http_request
import json
def get_mlflow_client():
    """Returns an initialized MLflowClient object."""
    return mlflow.tracking.client.MlflowClient()
```

```python
def get_host_creds(client):
    """Fetches host and token credentials."""
    return client._tracking_client.store.get_host_creds()
def mlflow_call_endpoint(endpoint, method, body='{}'):
    """Calls an MLflow REST API endpoint.
    Parameters:
        endpoint (str): The endpoint to call.
        method (str): HTTP method ('GET' or other HTTP methods).
        body (str): JSON-formatted request payload.
    Returns:
        dict: JSON response as a dictionary.
    """
    host_creds = get_host_creds(get_mlflow_client())

    try:
        if method == 'GET':
            response = http_request(
                host_creds=host_creds,
                endpoint=f"/api/2.0/mlflow/{endpoint}",
                method=method,
                params=json.loads(body)
            )
        else:
            response = http_request(
                host_creds=host_creds,
                endpoint=f"/api/2.0/mlflow/{endpoint}",
                method=method,
                json=json.loads(body)
            )

        return response.json()

    except Exception as e:
        print(f"Failed to call MLflow endpoint '{endpoint}': 
{str(e)}")
        return None
client = get_mlflow_client()
host_creds = get_host_creds(client)
host = host_creds.host
token = host_creds.token
```

2. In Command 16, assign the value of the slack_webhook variable to the webhook link for your Slack channel:

```
slack_webhook = "https://hooks.slack.com/servi
ces/????????/?????????/????????????????????"
```

3. Execute Command 17 and Command 18. This will register new webhooks for the model we registered for our **Customer Prediction Bank** problem. We will be notified when a new model version is created or a transition request has been made for a model version:

```
import json
trigger_for_slack = json.dumps({
  "model_name": registry_model_name,
  "events": ["MODEL_VERSION_CREATED"],
  "description": "Triggered when a new model version is
created.",
  "http_url_spec": {
    "url": slack_webhook
  }
})

mlflow_call_endpoint("registry-webhooks/create", method =
"POST", body = trigger_for_slack)
trigger_for_slack = json.dumps({
  "model_name": registry_model_name,
  "events": ["TRANSITION_REQUEST_CREATED"],
  "description": "Triggered when a new transition request for a
model has been made.",
  "http_url_spec": {
    "url": slack_webhook
  }
})
mlflow_call_endpoint("registry-webhooks/create", method =
"POST", body = trigger_for_slack)
```

4. The http_url_spec parameter is where you provide the URL for the HTTP webhook.

5. Now, after this point, if you go back to your model UI or request transitioning a model to a new stage, you will get notified in Slack:

Figure 6.17 – Automated notification received on Slack channel using Slack webhook

The notebook also demonstrates other REST API calls that can help you manage the webhooks.

We've just seen an example of how you can use webhooks for HTTP endpoints. Similarly, we can set up a job registry webhook. This can be used to trigger certain Databricks jobs you may have for testing a model or retraining a model version.

There are two parameters that you need to provide in job registry webhooks that are different from the HTTP registry webhooks: `job_spec` and `workspace_url`. You can kick off jobs in a workspace that is different from the one in the Model Registry. If you don't define `workspace_url`, then by default, the job specification will be used to trigger a Databricks job in the same workspace as the Model Registry.

Summary

In this chapter, we covered how you can utilize the Databricks Model Registry to manage ML model versioning and life cycles. We also learned how you can manage ML model versioning using the MLflow Model Registry and transition models from one stage to another while managing access control. We then learned how you can use MLflow-supported webhook callbacks to set up automated Slack notifications to track changes around models in your Model Registry.

In the next chapters, we will cover various model deployment approaches.

Further reading

The following are some links to further your understanding:

- Databricks, *Databricks AutoML*: `https://docs.databricks.com/applications/machine-learning/automl.html#databricks-automl`

- Databricks, *Job registry webhook example workflow*: `https://docs.databricks.com/applications/mlflow/model-registry-webhooks.html#job-registry-webhook-example-workflow`

- Slack, *Sending messages using incoming Webhooks*: `https://api.slack.com/messaging/webhooks#enable_webhook`

7

Model Deployment Approaches

In the previous chapter, we looked at how we can utilize Databricks MLflow Model Registry to manage our ML model versioning and life cycle. We also learned how we could use the integrated access control to manage access to the models registered in Model Registry. We also understood how we could use the available webhook support with Model Registry to trigger automatic Slack notifications or jobs to validate the registered model in the registry.

In this chapter, we will take the registered models from Model Registry and understand how to deploy them using the various model deployment options available in Databricks.

We will cover the following topics:

- Understanding ML deployments and paradigms
- Deploying ML models for batch and streaming inference
- Deploying ML models for real-time inference
- Incorporating custom Python libraries into MLflow models for Databricks deployment
- Deploying custom models with MLflow and Model Serving
- Packaging dependencies with MLflow models

Let's go through the technical requirements for this chapter.

Technical requirements

We'll need the following before diving into this chapter:

- Access to a Databricks workspace
- A running cluster with **Databricks Runtime for Machine Learning** (**Databricks Runtime ML**) with a version of 13 or above
- All the previous notebooks, executed as described
- A basic knowledge of Apache Spark, including DataFrames and SparkUDF

Let's take a look at what exactly ML deployment is.

Understanding ML deployments and paradigms

Data science is not the same as **data engineering**. Data science is more geared toward taking a business problem that we convert into data problems using scientific methods. We develop mathematical models and then optimize their performance. Data engineers are mainly concerned with the reliability of the data in the data lake. They are more focused on the tools to make the data pipelines scalable and maintainable while meeting the **service-level agreements (SLAs)**.

When we talk about ML deployments, we want to bridge the gap between data science and data engineering.

The following figure visualizes the entire process of ML deployment:

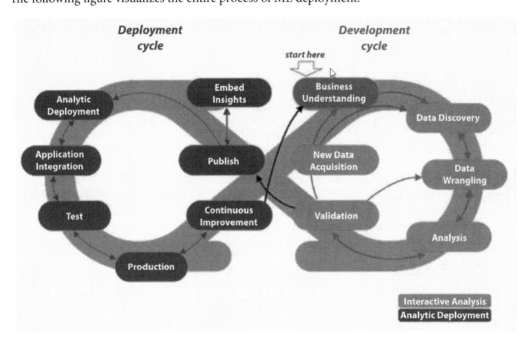

Figure 7.1 – Displaying the ML deployment process

On the right-hand side, we have the process of data science, which is very interactive and iterative. We understand the business problem and discover the datasets that can add value to our analysis. Then, we build data pipelines to wrangle the data and analyze it. We develop our models, and the chain continues.

The left-hand side of this diagram showcases the integration of the best practices from the software development world into the data science world. It's mostly automated. Once our candidate model is ready, we do the following:

1. First, we register it with the Model Registry.

2. Next, we integrate the model with our applications.

3. Then, we test the integrated model with our application.

4. Finally, we deploy it to production, where we monitor the model's performance and improve it.

Some of these processes may look very similar to DevOps, but there are some critical differences between **DevOps** and **ModelOps**.

DevOps, in essence, combines software development and IT operations such as **continuous integration (CI)**, **continuous deployment (CD)**, updating or rolling back features, and pushing a patch.

ModelOps combines the principles of DevOps, such as CI/CD, with specific requirements tailored to the world of ML. It introduces the need for continuous training and monitoring of ML models.

Continuous training is a vital aspect of ModelOps. Unlike traditional software, where once a module is deployed, it rarely changes, ML models require ongoing updates. With the influx of new data, models must be periodically retrained to ensure their accuracy and relevance. This means that even if the core model code remains unchanged, the model itself evolves to adapt to the changing data landscape.

Continuous monitoring in ModelOps encompasses two key areas: model performance monitoring and infrastructure monitoring. Model performance monitoring involves tracking how well the model is performing in real-world scenarios. This includes metrics such as accuracy, precision, and recall, among others. Infrastructure monitoring, on the other hand, focuses on the health and performance of the computing infrastructure supporting the model. This dual monitoring approach ensures that both the model and the underlying systems are operating optimally.

This approach differs from traditional software engineering, where once a software module is tested and deployed to production, it typically remains stable without the need for continuous monitoring and adaptation. In ModelOps, the ever-evolving nature of data and the importance of maintaining model performance make continuous training and monitoring integral components of the process.

In the initial days of MLOps, most companies used Java and custom-built in-house tools for managing ML deployments, continuous training, and monitoring. However, today, most of the tools and frameworks have become open source, and we have seen Python is the de facto standard when implementing the entire model development life cycle in production.

Let's take a look at the most common ML deployment paradigms. Most ML use cases can be categorized into four buckets:

- **Batch deployments** (run ad hoc or at a scheduled time):

  - These are the most common deployments and are relatively easy to implement and are most efficient in terms of cost and productionization effort.

  - Models make predictions that are stored in fast-access data repositories such as DynamoDB, Cassandra, Cosmos DB, or Delta tables within data lakehouses. These storage solutions are chosen for their efficiency in serving predictions. However, it's important to note that these choices are tailored to use cases with low-latency retrieval requirements, and batch use cases with less stringent retrieval time constraints may have different considerations. Additionally, Databricks SQL offers a serverless, high-performance data warehousing solution that seamlessly integrates with data lakehouses, simplifying data management and analytics for enhanced productivity and reliability in leveraging predictive models. It's worth mentioning that Delta tables also incorporate write optimizations, ensuring efficient data storage and processing.

- **Streaming deployments** (run continuously on the data):

  - These deployments become essential when you don't have access to your entire dataset before the inference starts, and you need to process new data relatively quickly as soon as it arrives.

  - Spark Structured Streaming is excellent for processing streaming data. It also has an inbuilt queuing mechanism, making it very useful when processing extensive image data.

- **Real time** (REST endpoint):

  - These deployments become important when the use cases require near real-time requests and responses from a model deployed as part of an application.

  - At the time of writing this book, Databricks boasts a production-grade model serving offering that's seamlessly integrated into its platform. This offering harnesses the power of serverless computing for optimal performance. Although delving into exhaustive details about the multitude of deployment architectures is not within the purview of this book, you can access comprehensive information on this subject in the Databricks documentation (`https://docs.databricks.com/en/serverless-compute/index.html`). Alternatively, you can seamlessly deploy your ML models as REST endpoints following their development and testing phases on Databricks with various cloud services such as Azure ML (leveraging Azure Kubernetes Service), AWS Sagemaker, and Google Vertex AI. The ML model is packaged into a container image and subsequently registered with the managed services offered by the respective cloud providers.

  - You can also use your own Kubernetes clusters for model deployments using the same paradigm.

- **On-device** (edge):

  - These are very specific use cases in which we want to deploy models on devices such as Raspberry Pis or other IoT use cases. We will not be covering these in this chapter.

As a best practice, it's advisable to initially consider batch deployment as your go-to ML deployment paradigm. Transition to alternative paradigms only after thoroughly validating that batch deployment is inadequate for your specific use case. Keep in mind that the long-term maintenance costs associated with a real-time ML deployment system are generally higher than those for a batch system.

It's also crucial to factor in response latency requirements when selecting the most appropriate ML deployment paradigm:

- **Batch deployment**: Ideally suited for scenarios where the expected response time for inference ranges from hours to days:

  - **Use case recommendation**: This is particularly useful for data analytics and reporting tasks that are not time-sensitive, such as generating monthly sales forecasts or risk assessments.

- **Structured streaming deployment**: Optimal for use cases requiring inference on new data within a time frame of a few minutes up to an hour:

  - **Use case recommendation**: Real-time analytics or fraud detection systems often benefit from this deployment type, where the data stream needs to be analyzed continuously but an instant response is not critical.

- **Near real-time or REST endpoint deployments**: These are suitable when the expected latency lies between hundreds of milliseconds to a minute:

  - **Use case recommendation**: This deployment paradigm is best suited for applications such as real-time recommendation systems or automated customer service bots, which require fairly quick responses but not immediate action.

- **Edge deployments**: These are geared toward scenarios demanding sub-100 ms SLAs:

  - **Use case recommendation**: This is crucial for **Internet of Things** (**IoT**) applications, autonomous vehicles, or any use case that requires lightning-fast decision-making capabilities.

There are just broad guidelines. The following figure summarizes all the points we discussed here:

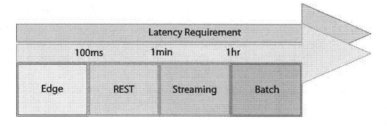

Figure 7.2 – The response latency requirements for various ML deployments

Now, let's look at the various deployment options when using Databricks. Apart from the deployment approaches discussed here, some open source projects may interest you for serving models as REST. The links to these can be found in the *Further reading* section at the end of this chapter.

Deploying ML models for batch and streaming inference

This section will cover examples of deploying ML models in a batch and streaming manner using Databricks.

In both **batch** and **streaming** inference deployments, we use the model to make the predictions and then store them at a location for later use. The final storage area for the prediction results can be a database with low latency read access, cloud storage such as S3 to be exported to another system, or even a Delta table that can easily be queried by business analysts.

When working with large amounts of data, Spark offers an efficient framework for processing and analyzing it, making it an ideal candidate to leverage our trained machine learning models.

> **Note**
> One important note to remember is that we can use any non-distributed ML library to train our models. So long as it uses the MLflow model abstractions, you can utilize all the benefits of MLflow's Model Registry and the code presented in this chapter.

We should always consider the access pattern of the results generated by the model. Depending on where we store our prediction results, we can perform the following optimizations:

- Partitioning, which can speed up data reads if your data is stored as static files or in a data warehouse
- Building indexes in databases on the relevant query, which generally improves performance

Let's look at an example of how to perform batch and stream inference deployment using the Databricks environment.

Batch inference on Databricks

Batch inference is the most common type of model deployment paradigm. Running inference in batch infers running predictions using a model and storing them for later use.

For this, we will use the model available to us in MLflow's Model Registry. We must ensure that we have at least one model version in staging for the notebook provided as part of this chapter to execute it:

1. Go into the **Models** tab and select the **Churn Prediction Bank** registered model. There should be a model version that is in the **Staging** state:

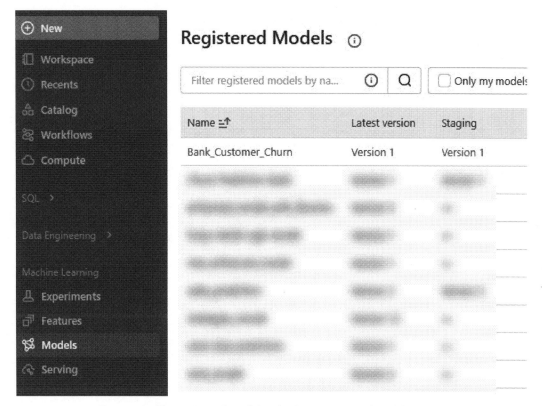

Figure 7.3 – The registered model in the Staging stage of Model Registry

2. Open the notebook associated with Chapter-07 named *Batch and Streaming*. We will simply load the model from the registry as a Python function, as shown in the following code block:

```
import mlflow
# the name of the model in the registry
registry_model_name = "Churn Prediction Bank"
# get the latest version of the model in staging and load it as
a spark_udf.
# MLflow easily produces a Spark user defined function
(UDF).  This bridges the gap between Python environments and
applying models at scale using Spark.
model = mlflow.pyfunc.spark_udf(spark, model_uri = f"models:/
{registry_model_name}/staging")
```

3. The rest of the notebook reads the same `raw_data` that we used to train our model in a Spark DataFrame and then after selecting the columns that we used to train our classification model using AutoML:

```
spark_df = spark.table("bank_churn_analysis.raw_Data")
display(spark_df)
exclude_colums = {'RowNumber', "CustomerId", "Surname",
"Exited"}
input_columns = [col for col in spark_df.columns if col not in
exclude_colums]
input_columns
# passing non label columns to the model as input
prediction_df = spark_df.withColumn("prediction", model(*input_
columns))
display(prediction_df)
```

Let's take a look at how we can utilize the same model loaded as a Spark UDF in a streaming inference deployment.

We won't get into the details about how Structured Streaming in Spark works in this chapter as it is a large topic in itself. *Spark: The Definitive Guide: Big Data Processing Made Simple* is a great book for learning in-depth about Apache Spark and Structured Streaming. A streaming DataFrame can be conceptualized as an unbounded table that continuously updates as new data arrives. Links have been provided in the *Further reading* section to different resources for you to learn more about Structured Streaming.

Streaming inference on Databricks

Let's look at the sample code to demonstrate how you can deploy the model we used in the previous section to perform streaming inference:

1. In `Cmd 15`, we must define `raw_data` from the Delta table to be read as a stream instead of a batch:

```
# right now we are just defining a streaming data source but
this statement will not execute until we call an Spark action.
Another way to exclude the columns that are not needed is by
dropping them from the DataFrame.
raw_streaming_df = spark.readStream.format("delta").
option("ignoreChanges", "true").table("bank_churn_analysis.raw_
Data").drop(*("RowNumber", "CustomerId", "Surname", "Exited"))
```

The rest of the flow will look similar to batch inference.

2. Once we have defined our streaming Dataframe, we call upon the same model that we loaded from the model registry that is available in the staging environment:

```
predictions_df = raw_streaming_df.withColumn("prediction",
model(*raw_streaming_df.columns))
display(predictions_df, streamName=stream_name)
```

Once we have predictions ready, we can write the data out as a Delta table or format that is efficient for our use case.

Now, let's take a look at how easy it is to use the same model if we want to perform real-time inference.

Deploying ML models for real-time inference

Real-time inferences include generating predictions on a small number of records using a model deployed as a REST endpoint. The expectation is to receive the predictions in a few milliseconds.

Real-time deployments are needed in use cases when the features are only available when serving the model and cannot be pre-computed. These deployments are more complex to manage than batch or streaming deployments.

Databricks offers integrated model serving endpoints, enabling you to prototype, develop, and deploy real-time inference models on production-grade, fully managed infrastructure within the Databricks environment. At the time of writing this book, there are two additional methods you can utilize to deploy your models for real-time inference:

- Managed solutions provided by the following cloud providers:

    - **Azure ML**

    - **AWS SageMaker**

    - **GCP VertexAI**

- Custom solutions that use Docker and Kubernetes or a similar set of technologies

If you're considering a robust solution for deploying and managing ML models in a production setting, Databricks Model Serving offers a host of compelling features:

- **Effortless endpoint creation**: With just a click, Databricks takes care of setting up a fully equipped environment suitable for your model, complete with options for serverless computing.

- **Adaptive scalability and reliability**: Built for the rigors of production, Databricks Model Serving is engineered to manage a high throughput of over 25,000 queries every second. The service dynamically scales to meet fluctuating demand and even allows the accommodation of multiple models on a single access point.

- **Robust security measures**: Every deployed model operates within a secure digital perimeter and is allocated dedicated computing resources that are decommissioned once the model is no longer in use.

- **Smooth integration with MLflow**: The platform easily hooks into MLflow's Model Registry, streamlining the deployment process of your ML models.

- **Comprehensive monitoring and debugging**: Databricks captures all request and response interactions in a specialized Delta table, facilitating real-time monitoring. Metrics such as query speed, latency, and error metrics are updated dynamically and are exportable to your choice of monitoring solution.

- **Real-time feature incorporation**: If you've trained your model using Databricks' Feature Store, those features are seamlessly bundled with the model. Furthermore, these can be updated in real time if you've configured your online feature store.

Let's understand some of the important technical details around the model serving endpoint feature grouped into various categories.

In-depth analysis of the constraints and capabilities of Databricks Model Serving

In this section, we will provide a comprehensive overview of the key technical aspects surrounding the use of Databricks Model Serving. From the payload size and query throughput limitations to latency and concurrency metrics, this section aims to equip you with essential insights that will guide your utilization of Databricks Model Serving effectively. Additionally, we will delve into system resource allocation details and discuss compliance and regional limitations that may impact your operations. Finally, we will touch upon miscellaneous factors and operational insights that could influence your decision-making when deploying ML models on this platform.

- **Payload constraints and query throughput**:

  - **Payload size**: It's worth noting that the payload size for each request is capped at 16 MB. For most standard use cases, this is sufficient, but for more complex models, optimizations may be required.

  - **Queries per second (QPS)**: The system comes with a default limit of 200 QPS per workspace. Although adequate for experimentation and low-traffic services, this can be scaled up to 25,000 QPS for high-demand scenarios by consulting Databricks support.

- **Latency and concurrency metrics**:

  - **Evaluation latency**: Those of us who work with computationally intensive models need to be mindful that Databricks imposes a 120-second upper limit for evaluation latency.

- **Concurrent requests**: Concurrency is capped at 200 queries per second across all serving endpoints in a workspace.. While this is often more than adequate, custom adjustments can be made through Databricks support for higher-demand services.

- **System resources and overhead**:

  - **Memory**: The environment allocates a default of 4 GB per model. This is generally sufficient for most traditional ML models, but deep learning models may require an extension of up to 16 GB.

  - **Latency overhead**: The architecture aims for a sub-50 ms additional latency, which is a best-effort approximation rather than a guarantee.

- **Compliance and regional restrictions**:

  - **HIPAA compliance**: For those in the healthcare domain, it's critical to note that Databricks Model Serving isn't currently HIPAA compliant.

  - **Regional limitations**: There are instances where workspace location can disrupt Model Serving capabilities. This is an essential factor to consider during the planning stage. For a list of supported regions, go to `https://docs.databricks.com/en/resources/supported-regions.html`.

- **Miscellaneous factors**:

  - **Initialization scripts**: Databricks Model Serving currently does not support initialization scripts, which may affect the deployability of certain specialized models.

  - **Model dependencies**: When serving AutoML-trained models, they may face dependency issues. An error like "*No module named* '`pandas.core.indexes.numeric`'" can occur due to incompatible pandas versions. To fix it:

    i.   Run '`add-pandas-dependency.py`' (`https://learn.microsoft.com/en-us/azure/databricks/_extras/documents/add-pandas-dependency.py`) script with the MLflow `run_id`.

    ii. Re-register the model in the MLflow model registry.

    iii. Serve the updated MLflow model.

- **Operational insights**:

  - **Endpoint creation time**: The time it takes to provision a new model endpoint is around 10 minutes.

  - **Zero-downtime updates**: The system is designed to perform endpoint updates with zero downtime, minimizing operational risk.

- **Dynamic scaling**: Databricks Model Serving employs intelligent scaling algorithms that adapt to fluctuating traffic patterns and provisioned concurrency, ensuring optimal resource allocation.

Let's take a look at an example of how you can use Databricks' inbuilt Model Serving endpoints to develop, prototype, and deploy models to generate real-time inference:

1. Go to the **Models** section in your workspace and select the **Churn Prediction Bank** model:

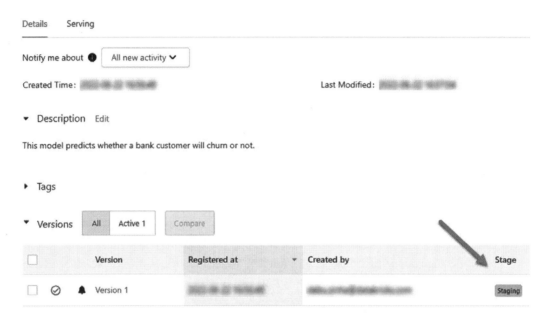

Figure 7.4 – The registered model in the Staging stage of Model Registry

2. Click on the **Use model for inference** button:

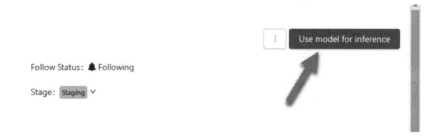

Figure 7.5 – The Use model for inference button, which gives you the option to either use the model for batch/streaming inference or as a real-time REST endpoint

3. Select **Real-time** and click on **Enable Serving**. Here, we can select what model version we want to serve and also the name of the serving endpoint. There are also options to automatically generate code for batch and streaming inference from the UI:

Figure 7.6 – How to enable real-time serving from the UI

4. You can also specify the type of compute resources you'd like to allocate for your model deployment. This is determined by the volume of concurrent requests that your endpoint is expected to handle. For our example, we will select **Small**:

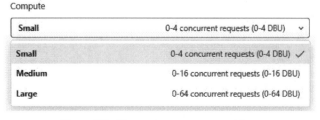

Figure 7.7 – The various compute options

5. Lastly, you can also select the **Scale to zero** option to make sure that your endpoint is not costing you when there is no load on it. Now, click **Create Endpoint**.

6. You will be redirected to the **Status** page, where you can see the current state of your model deployment, including what versions of the models are being deployed:

churn_prediction

Serving endpoint state: ⊘ Ready

Created by:

URL:

Tags: ✎

Active configuration

Model	Version	Name	State
■ Churn Prediction Bank	Version 1	Churn-Prediction-Bank-1	⊘ Ready

Figure 7.8 – The status page of the deployed Model Serving endpoint

7. You can also check the events associated with the model deployments:

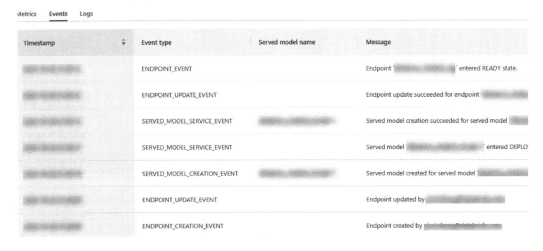

Timestamp	Event type	Served model name	Message
	ENDPOINT_EVENT		Endpoint ' ' entered READY state.
	ENDPOINT_UPDATE_EVENT		Endpoint update succeeded for endpoint
	SERVED_MODEL_SERVICE_EVENT		Served model creation succeeded for served model
	SERVED_MODEL_SERVICE_EVENT		Served model ' ' entered DEPLO
	SERVED_MODEL_CREATION_EVENT		Served model created for served model '
	ENDPOINT_UPDATE_EVENT		Endpoint updated by
	ENDPOINT_CREATION_EVENT		Endpoint created by

Figure 7.9 – The Status page of the deployed Model Serving endpoint

You can do the same for the metrics associated with the endpoint:

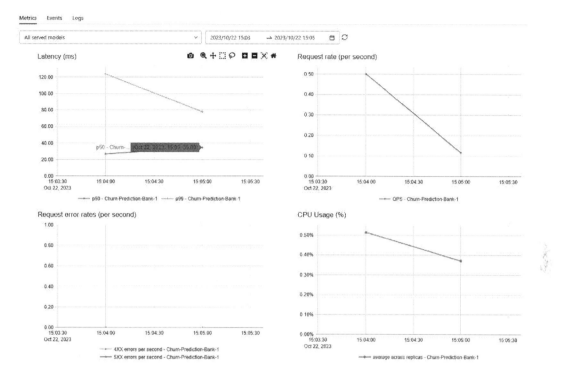

Figure 7.10 – The metrics associated with the Model Serving endpoint

Another important thing to note here is that access to the REST endpoint is inherited from the permissions you set in Model Registry:

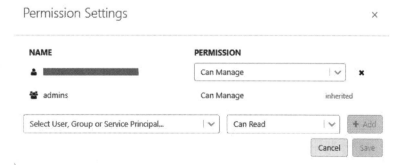

Figure 7.11 – The permissions inherited by the Model Serving endpoint

8. Now, let's take a look at how you can query your model. In the UI, once you see your model endpoint in the **Ready** state, you can click the **Query endpoint** button at the top-right corner of the serving endpoint status page:

Figure 7.12 – The Query endpoint button

There are code snippets that explain how to query a particular version of your deployed model either in Python, cURL, or SQL. There is another option to mimic a browser request and the following steps describe how you can utilize it:

1. Click on the **Show Example** button. This will only work when we have input examples logged in MLflow alongside the model:

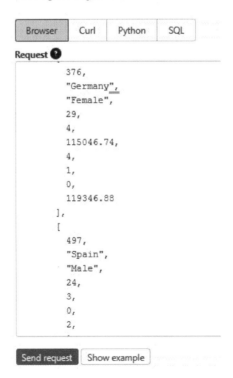

Figure 7.13 – The automatically logged sample input records from AutoML

2. To send the JSON request to our model for real-time inference, simply click **Send request**:

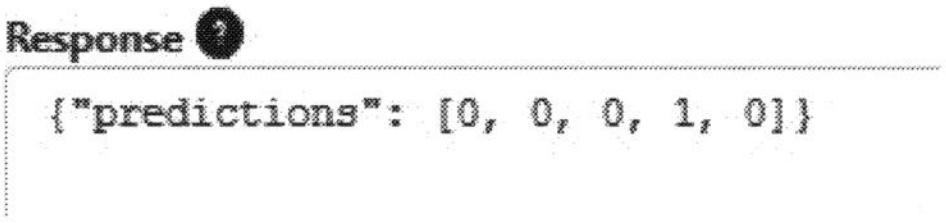

Response ❓
```
{"predictions": [0, 0, 0, 1, 0]}
```

Figure 7.14 – The response that was received from the deployed model

When we trained our Churn prediction model, AutoML logged example inputs that our model expects when deployed as a REST endpoint. If you are not using AutoML and training the model yourself, the MLflow API can be used to log sample inputs to your model at the time of a model run.

Let's look at how we can use Python to query the model endpoints with the help of the example notebook:

1. Open the `Real-Time` notebook in the `Chapter-07` folder.

2. To query the model endpoint, we need each REST call to be accompanied by a Databricks **Personal Access Token** (**PAT**). In `Cmd` 4, we must extract the PAT token from our notebook instance and programmatically extract our workspace domain name. This helps keep our code workspace-agnostic:

```
# get token from notebook
token = dbutils.notebook.entry_point.getDbutils().notebook().
getContext().apiToken().getOrElse(None)
#create authorization header for REST calls
headers = {
    "Authorization": f"Bearer {token}",
    "Content-Type": "application/json"
}

# Next we need an enpoint at which to execute our request which
we can get from the Notebook's tags collection
java_tags = dbutils.notebook.entry_point.getDbutils().
notebook().getContext().tags()
# This object comes from the Java CM
tags = sc._jvm.scala.collection.JavaConversions.
mapAsJavaMap(java_tags)
# extract the databricks instance (domain name) from the
dictionary
instance = tags["browserHostName"]
```

3. `Cmd` 6 contains a method score that takes as input sample records for inference as a Python dictionary, converts it into JSON, and sends a request to the deployed model. The model then responds with the predictions that are returned in JSON format:

```
# Import the requests library for HTTP communication
import requests
```

```
#change the model_serving endpoint name to the one you have
given.
model_serving_endpoint_name = "churn_prediction"
# Define the function 'score_model' which takes a dictionary as
an input
def score_model(data_json: dict):

    # Construct the URL for the model serving endpoint
    url = f"https://{instance}/serving-endpoints/{model_serving_
endpoint_name}/invocations"

    # Make an HTTP POST request to score the model
    response = requests.request(method="POST", headers=headers,
url=url, json=data_json)

    # Check if the request was successful (HTTP status code 200)
    if response.status_code != 200:
        # If not, raise an exception detailing the failure
        raise Exception(f"Request failed with status {response.
status_code}, {response.text}")

    # Return the JSON response from the model scoring endpoint
    return response.json()
```

4. To engage with the serving endpoint APIs effectively, you should assemble your JSON request payload according to one of the recognized formats. Each format offers distinct advantages and limitations. In our specific scenario, our ML model anticipates input in the form of a pandas DataFrame. Therefore, we have two optimal orientation options to structure our API query to the endpoint:

    I.   **DataFrame in split orientation**: For pandas DataFrames, you can use the `dataframe_split` method, serialized in JSON in a split orientation. This format is more bandwidth-efficient compared to records orientation but is a bit harder to read:

```
payload = {
  "dataframe_split": {
    "index": [1, 2],
    "columns": ["CreditScore", "Geography", "Gender",
"Age", "Tenure", "Balance", "NumOfProducts", "HasCrCard",
"IsActiveMember", "EstimatedSalary"],
    "data": [[619, "France", "Female", 42, 2, 0.0, 1, 1, 1,
101348.88], [608, "Spain", "Female", 41, 1, 83807.86, 1, 0, 1,
112542.58]]
  }
}
```

II.   **DataFrame in records orientation**: The `records` layout is another available choice for representing DataFrame data. It comes as a JSON object with each entry presenting a row in the DataFrame. This record is easy to read and is human-friendly, but it consumes more bandwidth as the column names are repeated for each record:

```
payload = {
    "record_dataframe": [
        {
            "CreditScore": 619,
            "Geography": "France",
            "Gender": "Female",
            "Age": 42,
            "Tenure": 2,
            "Balance": 0.0,
            "NumOfProducts": 1,
            "HasCrCard": 1,
            "IsActiveMember": 1,
            "EstimatedSalary": 101348.88
        },
        {
            "CreditScore": 608,
            "Geography": "Spain",
            "Gender": "Female",
            "Age": 41,
            "Tenure": 1,
            "Balance": 83807.86,
            "NumOfProducts": 1,
            "HasCrCard": 0,
            "IsActiveMember": 1,
            "EstimatedSalary": 112542.58
        }
    ]
}
```

5.   Lastly, you can simply call inference on these records:

```
score_model(payload)
{'predictions': [0, 0]}
```

When dealing with ML models such as those built in TensorFlow or PyTorch, which expect tensor inputs, you generally have two primary formatting options to consider for API requests: instances and input. Both the instances and input formats offer unique advantages and limitations that can significantly impact the design and performance of your ML solution.

Let's delve into each format's specifics to better understand how they can be optimally utilized:

- **Instances format for tensors**: The **instances** format is tailored for tensor data, accommodating tensors in a row-wise manner. This is an ideal choice when all input tensors share the same dimension at index 0. Essentially, each tensor in an instances list can be conceptually combined with other tensors with the same name across the list to form the complete input tensor for the model. This merging is only seamless if all tensors conform to the same 0-th dimension:

  - Single tensor:

    ```
    {"instances": [8, 9, 10]}
    ```

  - Multiple named tensors:

    ```
    { "instances": [ { "t1": "a", "t2": [1, 2, 3, 4, 5], "t3": [[1,
    2], [3, 4], [5, 6]] }, { "t1": "b", "t2": [6, 7, 8, 9, 10],
    "t3": [[7, 8], [9, 10], [11, 12]] } ] }
    ```

- **Input format for tensors**: The **input** format is another option that structures tensor data in a column-oriented manner. This format differs from instances in a crucial way: it allows for varying tensor instances across different tensor types. This is in contrast to the instances format, which requires a consistent number of tensor instances for each type.

Databricks' serving functionality provides the flexibility to deploy multiple models behind a single endpoint, a feature that's particularly useful for conducting A/B tests. Furthermore, you can allocate a specific percentage of total traffic among the various models housed behind the same endpoint. For more details on this, you can consult the official documentation (https://dpe-azure. docs.databricks.com/machine-learning/model-serving/serve-multiple-models-to-serving-endpoint.html#serve-multiple-models-to-a-model-serving-endpoint).

Adding another model to an existing endpoint is a straightforward process via the user interface. Simply navigate to the **Edit Configuration** section and select the **Add served model** option. From there, you'll be able to choose which model from the registry to deploy, specify its version, define the compute resources, and set the desired traffic allocation:

Figure 7.15 – How to add multiple models behind the same endpoint

There is a notebook in the `Chapter-07` folder called `real-time-additional` that contains code that demonstrates how we can set these endpoints using the API using Python programmatically. You can go through it at your own pace.

Now, let's delve into other prevalent scenarios related to model deployment. First on the list is incorporating custom user-defined functions and libraries when deploying models with MLflow.

Incorporating custom Python libraries into MLflow models for Databricks deployment

If your projects necessitate the integration of bespoke Python libraries or packages hosted on a secure private repository, MLflow provides a useful utility function, `add_libraries_to_model`. This feature allows you to seamlessly incorporate these custom dependencies into your models during the logging process, before deploying them via Databricks Model Serving. While the subsequent code examples demonstrate this functionality using scikit-learn models, the same methodology can be applied to any model type supported by MLflow:

1. **Upload dependencies and install them in the notebook**: The recommended location for uploading dependency files is **Databricks File System (DBFS)**:

    ```
    dbutils.fs.cp("local_path/to/your_dependency.whl", "dbfs:/path/
    to/your_dependency.whl")
    # Installing custom library using %pip
    %pip install /dbfs/path/to/your_dependency.whl
    ```

2. **Model logging with custom libraries**: After installing the required library and uploading its Python wheel file, you can log the model using `mlflow.sklearn.log_model()` with the `pip_requirements` or `conda_env` parameters to specify your dependencies:

    ```
    # Logging the model
    import mlflow.sklearn

    custom_requirements = ["scikit-learn", "numpy", "/dbfs/path/to/
    your_dependency.whl"]
    mlflow.sklearn.log_model(model, "sklearn-model", pip_
    requirements=custom_requirements)
    ```

3. **Add libraries to the model**: MLflow provides the `add_libraries_to_model()` function for embedding custom libraries alongside the model to ensure consistent environments:

    ```
    import mlflow.models.utils
    model_uri = "models:/<model-name>/<model-version>"
    mlflow.models.utils.add_libraries_to_model(model_uri)
    ```

4. **Model deployment**: Once the new model version, including the custom libraries, has been registered, you can proceed to deploy it with Databricks Model Serving.

You can read more about this on the MLflow website (`https://www.mlflow.org/docs/latest/python_api/mlflow.models.html?highlight=add_libraries#mlflow.models.add_libraries_to_model`).

Here is another end-to-end example. You can find the entire code in the `custom-python-libraries` notebook in the `Chapter-07` folder:

```
# Model URI for accessing the registered model
access_model_uri = "models:/enhanced_model_with_libraries/1"

# Add libraries to the original model run
add_libraries_to_model(access_model_uri)

# Example to add libraries to an existing run
prev_run_id = "some_existing_run_id"
add_libraries_to_model(access_model_uri, run_id=prev_run_id)

# Example to add libraries to a new run
with mlflow.start_run():
    add_libraries_to_model(access_model_uri)

# Example to add libraries and register under a new model name
with mlflow.start_run():
    add_libraries_to_model(access_model_uri, registered_model_
name="new_enhanced_model")
```

Moving on, in the following section, we'll delve into the intricacies of custom model development, exploring how specialized algorithms, unique data processing techniques, and enterprise-specific requirements can be seamlessly integrated into your MLflow deployments for enhanced performance and compliance.

Deploying custom models with MLflow and Model Serving

Deploying ML models often requires more than just making predictions. Many use cases demand additional capabilities, such as preprocessing inputs, post-processing outputs, or even executing custom logic for each request. Custom models in MLflow offer this level of flexibility, making it possible to integrate specialized logic directly alongside your models. This section will walk you through how to deploy such custom models with Model Serving.

MLflow custom models are particularly beneficial in the following scenarios:

- **Preprocessing needs**: When your model requires specific preprocessing steps before inputs can be fed into the prediction function.

- **Post-processing requirements**: When the raw outputs of your model need to be transformed or formatted for end user consumption.

- **Conditional logic**: If the model itself has per-request branching logic, such as choosing between different models or algorithms based on the input.

- **Fully custom code**: When you need to deploy an entirely custom code base alongside your model.

To create a custom model in MLflow, you need to write a `PythonModel` class that implements two essential functions:

- `load_context`: The `load_context` method is responsible for initializing components like model parameters or third-party modules that are crucial for the model but only need to be loaded once. This step enhances the performance during the model's prediction phase.

- `predict`: This function contains all the logic that executes each time an input request is made.

Here is some example code that defines a custom MLflow model class called `CustomModel` that was built using the `PythonModel` base class:

```
class CustomModel(mlflow.pyfunc.PythonModel):
    def load_context(self, context):
        self.model = torch.load(context.artifacts["model-weights"])
        from preprocessing_utils.my_custom_tokenizer import
CustomTokenizer
        self.tokenizer = CustomTokenizer(context.artifacts["tokenizer_
cache"])

    def format_inputs(self, model_input):
        # insert code that formats your inputs
        pass

    def format_outputs(self, outputs):
        predictions = (torch.sigmoid(outputs)).data.numpy()
        return predictions

    def predict(self, context, model_input):
        model_input = self.format_inputs(model_input)
        outputs = self.model.predict(model_input)
        return self.format_outputs(outputs)
```

Let's understand this code in more detail as it can easily be modified in the future for your use cases.

- `load_context(self, context)`: The load_context method initializes essential resources for our model to execute. The resources are loaded only once to optimize the inference phase. Let's understand the code inside this method in more detail.

  - `self.model = torch.load(context.artifacts["model-weights"])`: This line loads a PyTorch model from the artifacts and assigns it to the `self.model` attribute. The model weights are expected to be part of the artifacts under the `model-weights` key.

  - `from preprocessing_utils.my_custom_tokenizer import CustomTokenizer`: This line imports a custom tokenizer class.

  - `self.tokenizer = CustomTokenizer(context.artifacts["tokenizer_cache"])`: This line creates an instance of the imported `CustomTokenizer` class and initializes it using an artifact labeled `tokenizer_cache`. It is stored in the `self.tokenizer` attribute.

- `format_inputs(self, model_input)`: This method is designed to handle the formatting or preprocessing of model inputs. As of now, this function's code has not been implemented and is indicated by pass.

  As of now, this function's code has not been implemented and is indicated by pass.

- `format_outputs(self, outputs)`: This function is responsible for post-processing or formatting the raw outputs from the model.

  - `predictions = (torch.sigmoid(outputs)).data.numpy()`: This line applies the sigmoid activation function to the raw outputs and then converts the resulting tensor into a NumPy array

  - This function formats or post-processes the model's raw outputs

- `predict(self, context, model_input)`: Finally, we have the predict method that performs the following steps:

  - `model_input = self.format_inputs(model_input)`: This line calls the `format_inputs` function to format or preprocess the inputs

  - `outputs = self.model.predict(model_input)`: This line uses the pre-loaded PyTorch model to generate predictions

  - `return self.format_outputs(outputs)`: This line calls `format_outputs` to post-process the raw outputs before returning them

MLflow allows you to log custom models, complete with shared code modules from your organization. For instance, you can use the `code_path` parameter to log entire code bases that the model requires:

```
mlflow.pyfunc.log_model(CustomModel(), "model", code_path =
["preprocessing_utils/"])
```

The `mlflow.pyfunc.log_model(CustomModel()`, `"model"`, `code_path =` `["preprocessing_utils/"])` line uses MLflow's `log_model` method to log a custom Python model for later use, such as serving or sharing it with team members. Let's break down the function arguments:

- `CustomModel()`: This is an instance of the custom Python model class you've defined (such as the `CustomModel` class we saw earlier). This model will be logged and can be later retrieved from MLflow's Model Registry.

- `"model"`: This is the name you are giving to the logged model. It serves as an identifier that can be used when you are referring to this model in MLflow.

- `code_path = ["preprocessing_utils/"]`: This is a list of local file paths to Python files that the custom model depends on. In this case, it indicates that the code in the `preprocessing_utils` folder is necessary for the custom model to function correctly. This is especially useful when you want to include some preprocessing or utility code that is required to run the model. When you log the model, the code in this directory will be packaged alongside it. This ensures that you'll have all the necessary code when you load the model later.

So, when this function is executed, it logs your `CustomModel` class instance as a model with the name "model" in MLflow. It also packages any dependent code located in the `preprocessing_utils/` directory along with it. The resulting artifact can then be loaded and executed anywhere MLflow is available, and it will include both the model and its dependencies.

Once you log your custom model, it can be registered with MLflow Model Registry and then deployed to a Model Serving endpoint, just like any other model.

Let's look at an end-to-end example showcasing the use of custom models. The code uses the wine dataset, which is a classic and straightforward multi-class classification problem. Specifically, the dataset contains 178 wine samples from three different cultivars (types of grapes) in Italy. Each sample has 13 different features, such as Alcohol, Malic acid, and so on.

The aim is to predict which cultivar a particular wine sample belongs to based on these 13 features. In other words, given a new wine sample, the model will predict whether it belongs to `class_0`, `class_1`, or `class_2`, each representing one of the three cultivars. It also provides the probabilities of the sample belonging to each of these classes.

The code utilizes a decision tree classifier trained on a subset of the wine dataset (the training set). Once the model has been trained, it's wrapped in a custom Python class (`CustomModelWrapper`) to facilitate logging via MLflow.

Finally, the model is used to make predictions on new, unseen data (the test set). This code is available in the `custom-model` notebook in the `Chapter-07` folder:

```
# Custom model class
class CustomModelWrapper(mlflow.pyfunc.PythonModel):
```

```
    # Initialize the classifier model in the constructor
    def __init__(self, classifier_model):
        self.classifier_model = classifier_model

    # Prediction method
    def predict(self, context, model_data):
        # Compute the probabilities and the classes
        probs = self.classifier_model.predict_proba(model_data)
        preds = self.classifier_model.predict(model_data)
        # Create a DataFrame to hold probabilities and predictions
        labels = ["class_0", "class_1", "class_2"]
        result_df = pd.DataFrame(probs, columns=[f'prob_{label}' for
label in labels])
        result_df['prediction'] = [labels[i] for i in preds]

        return result_df
```

The preceding code defines a `CustomModelWrapper` class that inherits from `mlflow.pyfunc.PythonModel`. This class serves as a wrapper for a given classifier model. The `__init__` method initializes the classifier, while the `predict` method computes probabilities and class predictions. These are then returned as a pandas DataFrame, which includes both the probability scores for each class and the final predicted labels:

```
# Load the wine dataset and split it into training and test sets
wine_data = load_wine()
X, y = wine_data.data, wine_data.target
X_train, X_test, y_train, y_test = train_test_split(X, y, test_
size=0.3, random_state=7)

# Initialize and fit the DecisionTreeClassifier
dt_classifier = DecisionTreeClassifier(random_state=7)
dt_classifier.fit(X_train, y_train)

# Create an instance of the CustomModelWrapper
custom_wrapper = CustomModelWrapper(dt_classifier)

# Define the input and output schema
input_cols = [ColSpec("double", feature) for feature in wine_data.
feature_names]
output_cols = [ColSpec("double", f'prob_{cls}') for cls in wine_data.
target_names] + [ColSpec("string", 'prediction')]
model_sign = ModelSignature(inputs=Schema(input_cols),
outputs=Schema(output_cols))
```

```
# Prepare an example input
input_sample = pd.DataFrame(X_train[:1], columns=wine_data.feature_
names)
input_sample_dict = input_sample.to_dict(orient='list')

# Log the model using MLflow
with mlflow.start_run():
    mlflow.pyfunc.log_model("wine_model",
                            python_model=custom_wrapper, input_
example=input_sample_dict, signature=model_sign)
```

Continuing from the custom model wrapper, this code takes additional steps to prepare for model deployment. First, it loads the wine dataset and divides it into training and test sets. `DecisionTreeClassifier` is then initialized and trained on the training set. Subsequently, an instance of `CustomModelWrapper` is created to encompass the trained classifier, adding an extra layer for output formatting.

The next phase involves defining the input and output schemas by specifying the data types and names of the features and target variables. These schemas serve as a blueprint for the model's expected input and output, which is crucial for later deployment stages. An example input is also crafted using a single row from the training set to illustrate how the model will receive data.

Finally, the model is logged into MLflow, incorporating not just the custom wrapper, but also the input example and the predefined schemas. This comprehensive logging ensures that the model is ready for future tracking and deployment with all its nuances intact.

In an ML deployment pipeline, ensuring that all model dependencies are correctly packaged is critical for stable, scalable, and efficient operation. The following section elaborates on the best practices for packaging these dependencies alongside your model using MLflow.

Packaging dependencies with MLflow models

In a Databricks environment, files commonly reside in DBFS. However, for enhanced performance, it's recommended to bundle these artifacts directly within the model artifact. This ensures that all dependencies are statically captured at deployment time.

The `log_model()` method allows you to not only log the model but also its dependent files and artifacts. This function takes an `artifacts` parameter where you can specify paths to these additional files:

```
Here is an example of how to log custom artifacts with your models:
mlflow.pyfunc.log_model(
    artifacts={'model-weights': "/dbfs/path/to/file", "tokenizer_
cache": "./tokenizer_cache"}
)
```

In custom Python models logged with MLflow, you can access these dependencies within the model's code using the `context.artifacts` attribute:

```
class CustomMLflowModel(mlflow.pyfunc.PythonModel):
    def load_context(self, context):
        self.model = torch.load(context.artifacts["model-weights"])
        self.tokenizer = transformers.BertweetTokenizer.from_
pretrained(
            "model-base",
            local_files_only=True,
            cache_dir=context.artifacts["tokenizer_cache"]
        )
```

At the time of serving the custom models from model endpoints, all the artifacts are copied over to the deployment container. They can be accessed as shown in the example using the context object.

MLflow allows you to specify a Conda environment for your model. You can provide a `conda.yaml` file that lists all the dependencies required by your model. When you serve the model, MLflow uses this Conda environment to ensure that all dependencies are correctly installed. This file is created automatically if you don't specify it manually at the time of logging the model.

Here's an example of how to specify a Conda environment in Python:

```
mlflow.pyfunc.log_model(
    python_model=MyModel(),
    artifact_path="my_model",
    conda_env={
        'name': 'my_custom_env',
        'channels': ['defaults'],
        'dependencies': [
            'numpy==1.19.2',
            'pandas==1.2.3',
            'scikit-learn==0.24.1',
        ],
    }
)
```

This brings us to the end of this chapter. Let's summarize what we've learned.

Summary

This chapter covered the various deployment options in Databricks for your ML models. We also learned about the multiple deployment paradigms and how you can implement them using the Databricks workspace. The book's subsequent editions will detail the many new features that Databricks is working on to simplify the MLOps journey for its users.

In the next chapter, we will dive deeper into Databricks Workflows to schedule and automate ML workflows. We will go over how to set up ML training using the Jobs API. We will also take a look at the Jobs API's integration with webhooks to trigger automated testing for your models when a model is transitioned from one registry stage to another.

Further reading

Here are some more links for further reading:

- *MLeap* (https://combust.github.io/mleap-docs)
- *Databricks, Introduction to DataFrames – Python* (https://docs.databricks.com/spark/latest/dataframes-datasets/introduction-to-dataframes-python.html)
- *Structured Streaming Programming Guide* (https://spark.apache.org/docs/latest/structured-streaming-programming-guide.html)
- Docker (https://docs.docker.com/)
- *Kubernetes* (https://kubernetes.io/docs/home/)
- *Pickle – Python object serialization* (https://docs.python.org/3/library/pickle.html)

8
Automating ML Workflows Using Databricks Jobs

In the last chapter, we covered the ML deployment life cycle and the various model deployment paradigms. We also understood how the response latency, the scalability of the solution, and the way we are going to access the predictions play an important role in deciding the deployment method.

In this chapter, we are going to take a look at **Databricks Workflows** with **Jobs** (previously called **Databricks Jobs**). This functionality can be leveraged not only to schedule the retraining of our models at regular intervals but also to trigger tests to check our models when transitioning from one **Model Registry** stage to another using the webhook integrations we discussed in *Chapter 6*.

We will be covering the following topics:

- Understanding Databricks Workflows
- Utilizing Databricks Workflows with Jobs to automate model training and testing

Technical requirements

The following are the technical requirements for this chapter:

- Access to the Databricks workspace with **Unrestricted cluster creation** permission at a minimum
- All the previous notebooks, executed as described

Now, let's take a look at Databricks Workflows.

Understanding Databricks Workflows

Workflows in the simplest sense are frameworks for developing and running your data processing pipelines.

Databricks Workflows provides a reliable, fully managed orchestration service for all your data, analytics, and AI workloads on the **Databricks Lakehouse** platform on any cloud. Workflows are designed to ground up with the Databricks Lakehouse platform, providing deep monitoring capabilities along with centralized observability across all your other workflows. There is no additional cost to customers for using Databricks Workflows.

The key benefit of using workflows is that users don't need to worry about managing orchestration software and infrastructure. Users can simply focus on specifying the business logic that needs to be executed as part of the workflows.

Within Databricks Workflows, there are two ways you can make use of the managed workflows:

- **Delta Live Tables (DLT)**: DLT is a declarative ETL framework to develop reliable pipelines on the Databricks Lakehouse platform. DLT allows easy monitoring of the ETL pipelines while managing the infrastructure needed to run these pipelines. It also has built-in expectations to allow validation of incoming data for each Delta table and keeps track of data lineage while providing data quality checks. DLT provides granular lineage at the table level and provides unified monitoring and alerting for all the parts of an ETL pipeline.

  DLT is an advanced topic in itself. Going into a lot of detail about DLT is outside the scope of this book. We will provide a link to get started with DLT in the *Further reading* section.

  The following figure illustrates what capabilities are wrapped inside DLT:

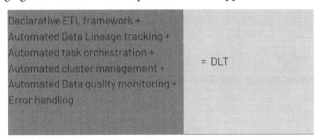

Figure 8.1 – All the capabilities that DLT provides

> **Note**
>
> Delta Pipelines are for pure declarative ETL. You cannot make API calls or send an email with them. You should use Delta pipelines for ETL. For everything else, use Workflows with Jobs. We will cover Workflows with Jobs in the next section from the perspective of triggering automated model retraining at regular intervals and performing automated validations on updated models in the Model Registry.

- **Workflows with Jobs**: A Job is a way we can use to trigger the execution of Databricks notebooks, libraries, and more, either immediately or at a fixed schedule. We will be covering this in more detail in this chapter from the perspective of automating your ML workflow.

As with almost all Databricks features, you can create Jobs either through the UI, **command-line interface** (**CLI**), or API. You can define one or more tasks as part of a Workflow with Jobs. A task can entail executing one of the following options:

- A **Databricks notebook** that is either in a Git repository that's accessible in your Databricks workspace or in a location in your workspace

- A **Python script** loaded in cloud storage and available through the **Databricks file system** (**DBFS**)

- **Java code compiled as a JAR file**, which should be installed on the cluster for this option to work

- A **DLT** pipeline

- A **spark-submit** command, which is a utility that allows the submission of Spark or PySpark application programs to the underlying cluster

- A **Python wheel**

You can chain multiple tasks together as part of a Job and repair and re-run a failed or canceled job. Databricks also provides support for monitoring the status of Jobs through the UI, CLI, API, and email notifications. Links will be provided in the *Further reading* section if you want to learn more about how to create and manage Workflows with Jobs using API or CLI. Jobs is a very versatile workflow management tool that can be used to develop and chain together tasks related to your ETL data pipeline or various steps in your ML workflows.

Let's delve into how you can automate the retraining of your machine learning models at regular intervals using the *Workflows with Jobs* feature in Databricks. Workflows offer fine-grained access control, allowing owners and administrators to grant permissions to other users or groups for viewing workflow run results and managing the workflow runs themselves. Next, we'll dive deeper into how to utilize Databricks Workflows with Jobs for automating both model training and testing.

Utilizing Databricks Workflows with Jobs to automate model training and testing

In this section, we'll delve into the powerful synergy between Databricks Workflows and Jobs to automate the training and testing of machine learning models. Before we jump into hands-on examples, it's essential to understand the significance of automation in the ML life cycle and how Databricks uniquely addresses this challenge.

Automating the training and testing phases in machine learning is not just a convenience but a necessity for scalable and efficient ML operations. Manual processes are not only time-consuming but also prone to errors, making automation a critical aspect of modern MLOps.

This is where Databricks Workflows comes in and allows for the orchestration of complex ML pipelines.

Let's take a look into an example workflow that we will automate using Workflows with Jobs. We will be going through the following logical steps shown in *Figure 8.2*:

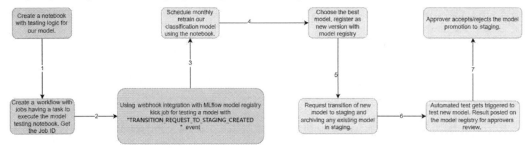

Figure 8.2 – A sample workflow of automated testing and alerting on new model promotions

All the relevant code for this part is in the `Chaper-08` folder. Let's take a look at how we can schedule a Databricks notebook as a Workflow with Jobs:

1. We first navigate to the [Workflows] tab in the left navigation bar. Here, we can click **Create Job**:

Figure 8.3 – The contents of the Databricks Workflows tab

2. Here, we can provide a name to the task, and then select **Notebook** under **Type**. In **Source**, we have two options – **Workspace** and **Git provider**:

    •   **Workspace**: Using the file browser, you can navigate to the notebook in the workspace you want to schedule as a task:

Select Notebook   ×

- Repos
- Shared
- Users

Cancel   Confirm

Figure 8.4 – How to browse a notebook for scheduling as a Job through exploring the Workspace option

You can simply navigate to the notebook in the Repos folder, as shown in the following screenshot, and hit **Confirm**:

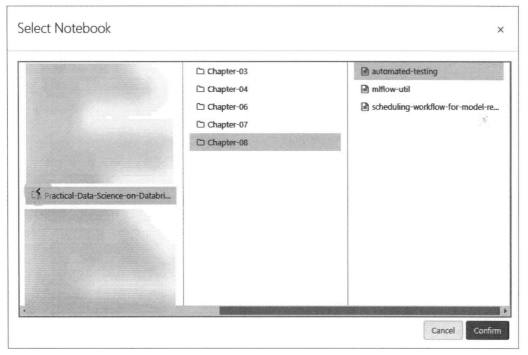

Figure 8.5 – How to browse a notebook for scheduling as a Job through the Repos functionality

> **Note**
>
> One important thing to keep in mind here is that when you use the Repos feature of Databricks, it creates a local copy for your repository or a clone. If you change code in the repository without performing a Git-pull of the latest version in your local repository, your updates will not make their way to the Job that you are scheduling with the current version of the repository code.
>
> For production deployments, it's important to make use of the Git provider as the source rather than the workspace as the source.

- **Git provider**: This method simplifies the creation and management of Jobs during productionizing and automated deployments. The main benefit here is that you can version control your data pipelines without managing permissions across multiple code repositories. You will also have a single source of truth for your model pipelines. Every time the Job executes, it will pull the latest version of the notebook/code from the remote repository with the specified branch or tag. Databricks supports the following Git providers: GitHub, Bitbucket Cloud, GitLab, Azure DevOps (excluding Azure China regions), AWS CodeCommit, and GitHub AE.

> **Note**
>
> An important thing to keep in mind is that if you use the Git provider option as the source of one of your notebooks that will be scheduled as a task, you cannot mix and match it with tasks that have notebooks using a workspace as their Source as part of the same Job workflow. This limitation is only for using the Databricks notebooks.

To add the notebook from a Git provider, enter the details of the repository you want to access the notebook from. In our case, I will use my own Git repository for this book as an example.

For **Path**, a couple of things need to be kept in mind:

- You need to enter a path relative to the notebook location
- Don't add a / or . / character at the beginning of the notebook path
- Don't include the file extension, such as .py
- For adding information about your Git repository, click on **Add a git reference**, which will open the following window pictured in *Figure 8.6* where you can select your Git provider.
- You can select to execute notebooks from a particular Git branch/tag or commit. In my case, I will be using the master branch:

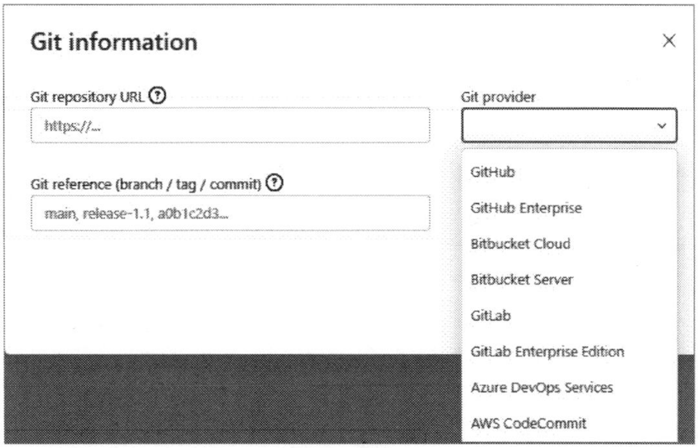

Figure 8.6 – How to set up a Databricks notebook to execute as a Job from the repository

When choosing the cluster, you can either utilize the cluster that is already up and running in your workspace or define a new Jobs cluster for all the tasks of the workflow. We have covered the difference between the cluster types in *Chapter 2*.

3. Lastly, you can also pass the parameters to your tasks. In notebooks, parameters are passed as notebook widgets.

    If you have a use case where you need to set up a JAR, `spark-submit` command, Python file, or Python wheel as a task, you can define the input parameters as a JSON-formatted array of strings. For Python tasks, the passed parameters can be accessed using the `argparse` (`https://docs.python.org/3/library/argparse.html`) Python module. For Python wheel tasks, you also have the option to pass in keyword arguments as key/value pairs that you can then access using the `argparse` package.

4. In the **Advanced Options** tab, you have optional settings to include **Dependent Libraries, Retry Policy in case of an error**, and **Timeouts**. You can additionally add users or groups of users to notify via email in case a task starts, succeeds, or fails. This setting is also available at the workflow level.

    For each workflow, you can also define the **Maximum concurrent** runs, which has a default value of `1`. This setting is important in cases where you may require to have overlapping execution of a particular Workflow with Jobs. A request to execute a Workflow with Jobs is skipped if the concurrent running instances of the workflow that is being requested to be executed have hit the maximum number of concurrent runs.

    In our case, we don't have any dependent task on our notebook task, so we will simply hit **Create**. You can also add multiple interdependent tasks as part of a workflow by clicking the (+ Add task) icon.

Once we have successfully created a task to execute as part of our workflow, we can see information about our workflow in the **Jobs** tab of the *Workflows* section. Now, we have the option to schedule the running of our workflow at regular intervals automatically or interactively using the **Run now** button.

We can see a graph showing the success and failure of the past executions of the workflows along with the runtime and the details of our Workflow with Jobs on the right-hand side. Take note of **Job ID**, as this will be used to automatically trigger our model testing notebook using the webhooks integration with the Model Registry:

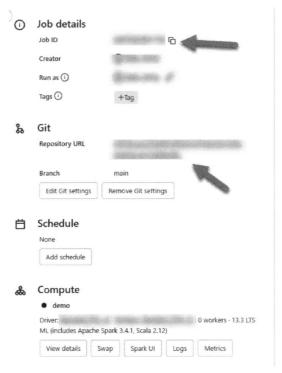

Figure 8.7 – The summary page to monitor the Job run history as well as the
unique Job ID, Git, Schedule, Compute, and Notifications settings

Let's take a look at the contents of the automated testing notebook in the `Chapter-08` folder that we just scheduled:

- `Cmd 2` is simply capturing the value of the `event_message` parameter that is sent by the Model Registry webhook. It contains information about the event that triggered the execution of this notebook workflow, such as the following:

  - `event_timestamp`: Time when the event occurred

  - `event`: Name of the event, as described in the chapter on webhooks

  - `text`: Description of the purpose of the webhook that initiated the automated test execution

  - `to_stage`: Target stage for the model to be transitioned to

- version: Model version whose transition triggered this webhook

- from_stage: Initial stage of the model version in the Model Registry

Depending on what type of task we are scheduling, the payload of the webhooks changes. There will be a link in the *Further reading* section if you want to learn more. The following code snippet demonstrates the process of retrieving and parsing the payload from webhooks:

```
import json
event_message = dbutils.widgets.get("event_message")
event_message_dict = json.loads(event_message)
model_name = event_message_dict.get("model_name")
print(event_message_dict)
print(model_name)
```

- Cmd 4 is simply running some utility code to interact with the MLflow REST API. It is a good practice to write modularized code for writing unit tests for your code:

```
import mlflow
from mlflow.utils.rest_utils import http_request
import json

def client():
    return mlflow.tracking.client.MlflowClient()

host_creds = client()._tracking_client.store.get_host_creds()
host = host_creds.host
token = host_creds.token

def mlflow_endpoint(endpoint, method, body='{}'):
    if method == 'GET':
        response = http_request(
            host_creds=host_creds, endpoint="/api/2.0/mlflow/
{}".format(endpoint), method=method, params=json.loads(body))
    else:
        response = http_request(
            host_creds=host_creds, endpoint="/api/2.0/mlflow/
{}".format(endpoint), method=method, json=json.loads(body))
    return response.json()
```

- In Cmd 7, we are downloading a specific model version from the MLflow Model Registry for running our tests:

```
import mlflow
pyfunc_model = mlflow.pyfunc.load_model(model_uri=f"models:/
{model_name}/{version}")
```

The rest of the code displays how you can write arbitrary tests to test your model before promoting it to the target stage in the Model Registry. In the sample code, we are testing whether the model being tested has the required schema for the inputs or not. We are also testing the output data type for the response.

At the end of successfully running the test, we send a message back to the Model Registry reporting whether all the tests passed or failed for the ML engineer to review:

```
# Leave a comment for the ML engineer who will be reviewing the tests
comment = "This model passed all the tests"
comment_body = {'name': model_name, 'version': version, 'comment':
comment}
mlflow_endpoint('comments/create', 'POST', json.dumps(comment_body))
```

With this, we are now ready to register the automated-test workflow with our model training notebook.

Let's take a look at the model training code. Open the scheduling-workflow-for-model-retraining notebook.

This notebook has code to first register a Jobs webhook with the TRANSITION_REQUEST_TO_STAGING_CREATED event trigger for our Churn Prediction Bank model in the Model Registry.

Let's look at the important cells in the notebook one by one:

1. In Cmd 2, we are simply installing a notebook-scoped databricks-registry-webhooks library from **Python Package Index (PyPI)**. This is an alternate way to interact with the Databricks Model Registry webhooks other than using the Databricks REST API we covered in *Chapter 6*.

2. In Cmd 3, we are simply reading our original raw_data table from the bank_churn_analysis table while excluding the features that we will not use to train our model.

3. Cmd 5 is some utility code that is dynamically extracting the token and our current workspace URL. This code can be put into its own segregated function to make it easy for testing.

4. In Cmd 7, we are registering the Job workflow we created in *step 1* to be triggered by a webhook on the TRANSITION_REQUEST_TO_STAGING_CREATED event. In the code, replace <jobid> with the Job Id you noted down in *step 2*:

```
from databricks_registry_webhooks import RegistryWebhooksClient,
JobSpec
job_spec = JobSpec(
  job_id="<jobid>",
  workspace_url="https://"+instance,
  access_token=token
)
job_webhook = RegistryWebhooksClient().create_webhook(
  model_name=model_name,
```

```
    events=["TRANSITION_REQUEST_TO_STAGING_CREATED"],
    job_spec=job_spec,
    description="Registering webhook to automate testing of a new
candidate model for staging"
)
job_webhook
```

5. Next, we use the `AutoML` Python API to trigger a model retraining job, with our primary metric being the `F1` score:

```
import databricks.automl
model = databricks.automl.classify(
    new_data.select(features),
    target_col=target_column,
    primary_metric="f1",
    timeout_minutes=5,
    max_trials=30,
)
```

6. Next, we simply use the `MLflowClient` class object to register the best-performing model into our Model Registry:

```
import mlflow
from mlflow.tracking.client import MlflowClient
client = MlflowClient()
run_id = model.best_trial.mlflow_run_id
model_uri = f"runs:/{run_id}/model"
model_details = mlflow.register_model(model_uri, model_name)
```

7. We now import some utility code that is just a wrapper on top of the `MLflow REST API` using the `%run` magic command. This is how you can modularize your code for easy testing and maintainability:

```
%run ./mlflow-util
```

8. In `Cmd 17`, we request transitioning the new model version to Staging. Since the new model needs to be tested first before we retire our old model, we are not going to archive the existing model version in Staging just yet. The following code block demonstrates the same.

```
staging_request = {'name': model_name, 'version': model_details.
version, 'stage': 'Staging', 'archive_existing_versions':
'false'}
mlflow_endpoint('transition-requests/create', 'POST', json.
dumps(staging_request))
```

9.   Lastly, we are also going to add a comment for the ML engineer to say that the model is ready for testing:

```
comment = "This was the best model from the most recent AutoML
run. Ready for testing"
comment_body = {'name': model_name, 'version': model_details.
version, 'comment': comment}
mlflow_endpoint('comments/create', 'POST', json.dumps(comment_
body))
```

With this, we can see that in the **Models** tab for our `Churn Prediction Bank` model, there is a new version of a registered model with a pending request.

We can get even more detail about this model by clicking the **Model** version. This will show us the request to transition the model and also the comment left after the model training:

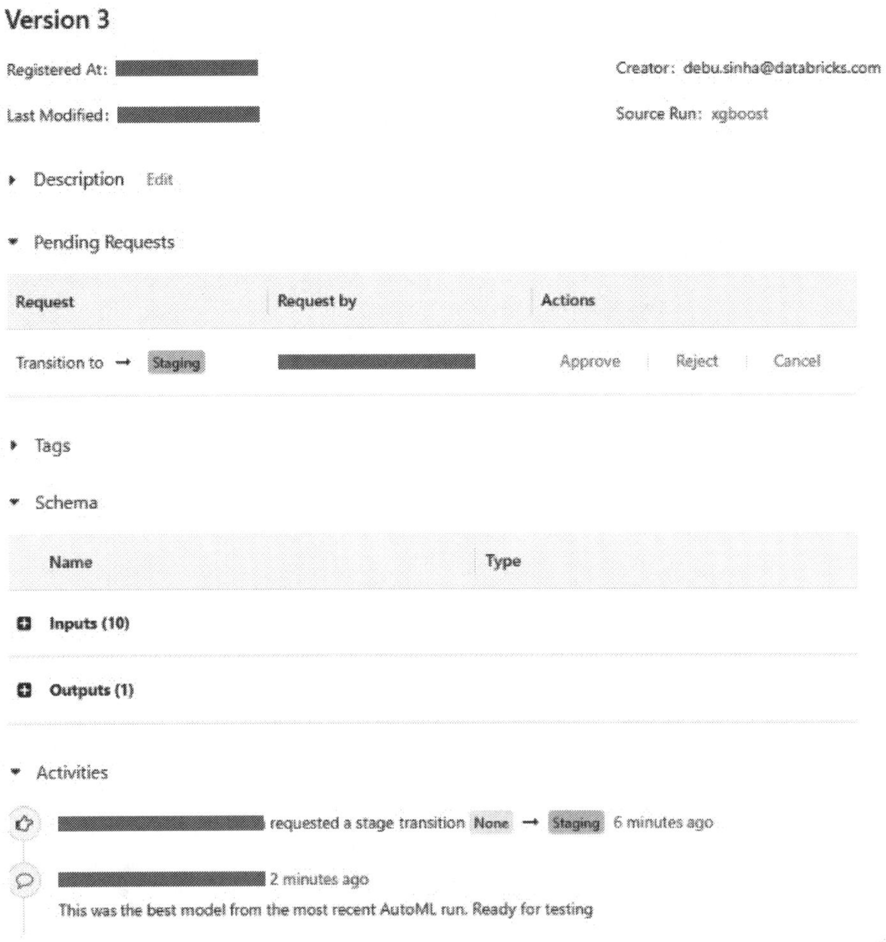

Version 3

Registered At: ▉▉▉▉▉▉▉▉▉▉   Creator: debu.sinha@databricks.com

Last Modified: ▉▉▉▉▉▉▉▉▉▉   Source Run: xgboost

▸ Description   Edit

▾ Pending Requests

Request	Request by	Actions		
Transition to → Staging	▉▉▉▉▉▉▉▉▉▉▉▉▉▉▉▉	Approve	Reject	Cancel

▸ Tags

▾ Schema

Name	Type
Inputs (10)	
Outputs (1)	

▾ Activities

◯ ▉▉▉▉▉▉▉▉▉▉▉▉▉ requested a stage transition None → Staging 6 minutes ago

◯ ▉▉▉▉▉▉▉▉▉▉▉▉▉ 2 minutes ago
   This was the best model from the most recent AutoML run. Ready for testing

Figure 8.8 – The message that we created using API to request model transition to Staging

10. On requesting the transition, we can see that the automated test is now executing on our new model version. We can see more details by clicking `automated_test`:

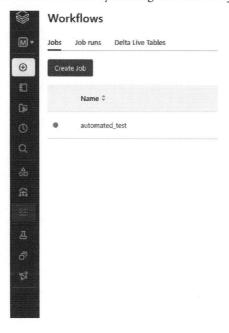

Figure 8.9 – The automated testing Job for any new model that gets a request to be transitioned to Staging

The matrix view shows the current status of our test. We can see the actual output of our test:

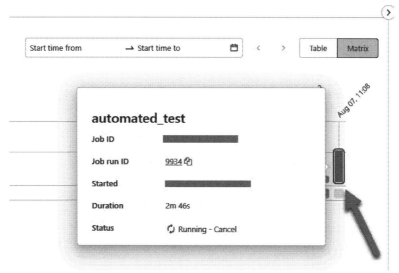

Figure 8.10 – The matrix view for our automated testing Job run

11. On successful completion of the model testing, we can check the status on the *model version* page:

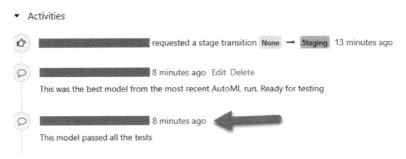

Figure 8.11 – The successful posting of the message into the Model
Registry after successful testing of the new model

12. Now, the ML engineer or the admin can archive the old model and approve the request to transition this model to the Staging environment.

In my case, that means transitioning the model version 2 to **Archived**:

Figure 8.12 – How to transition the existing model in Staging to Archived

13. We can add a comment that can keep track of why this model is being archived, which will also be logged in this model version's activity:

Figure 8.13 – How to add a message to the model being Archived action

14. Now I can approve the model version 3 transition to Staging and add a comment. We can approve the transition of the model to Staging and the retiring of the old model in Staging when we click on the **Approve** button:

Figure 8.14 – How to approve transitioning of the new model to Staging

This is useful in cases where you have only one version of a model in Staging at a given time. The explicit retiring can be useful if you want to have simultaneous candidate models in a stage for A/B testing before selecting the best model.

So, now we have executed the end-to-end workflow where we trained a new model and also triggered automated testing before promoting the model to Staging.

The last thing to do here is to schedule the monthly retraining of our model.

15. Go back to the `scheduling-workflow-for-model-retraining` notebook and open it. On the top right of every Databricks notebook, you have a button called **Schedule**. On clicking that, you can specify how often you want to execute this notebook and what type of cluster to execute it on. You can also add parameters for the notebook and set alerts:

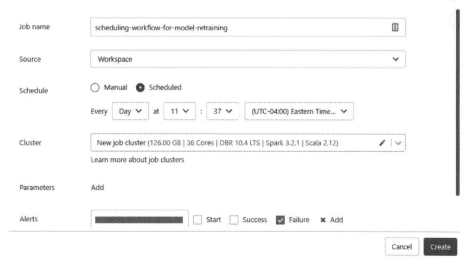

Figure 8.15 – How to set up our model for automated retraining

As we've explored the intricacies of automating machine learning workflows using Databricks Jobs, you should now have a solid understanding of how to set up and manage your automated ML retraining workflows. Next, we'll summarize the key takeaways in the *Summary* section to help you consolidate your knowledge.

Summary

In this chapter, we discussed the workflow management options available in the Databricks environment. We also looked at Workflows with Jobs functionality in more detail in relation to its utility in automating your ML workflows.

We went through a sample workflow of creating a notebook with tests to perform on any new model we want to transition to the Staging stage of the Model Registry. We then configured the Model Registry Jobs webhooks feature to be triggered by another automated model retraining notebook. Similar workflows can make your model tests arbitrarily complex to fit your needs.

In the last chapter, we will cover the concept of model drift and how to trigger a model's retraining automatically.

Further reading

Here are some links to further your understanding:

- Databricks, *What Is Delta Live Tables?*: `https://docs.databricks.com/en/delta-live-tables/index.html`

- Databricks, *Introduction to Databricks Workflows*: `https://docs.databricks.com/en/workflows/index.html`

9

Model Drift Detection and Retraining

In the last chapter, we covered various workflow management options available in Databricks for automating **machine learning** (**ML**) tasks. Now, we will expand upon our understanding of the ML life cycle up to now and introduce the fundamental concept of **drift**. We will discuss why model monitoring is essential and how you can ensure your ML models perform as expected over time.

At the time of writing this book, Databricks has a product that is in development that will simplify monitoring model performance and data out of the box. In this chapter, we will go through an example of how to use the existing Databricks functionalities to implement drift detection and monitoring.

We will be covering the following topics:

- Motivation for model monitoring

- Introduction to model drift

- Introduction to Statistical Drift

- Techniques for drift detection

- Implementing drift detection on Databricks

Let's go through the technical requirements for this chapter.

Technical requirements

The following are the prerequisites for the chapter:

- Access to a Databricks workspace

- A running cluster with Databricks Runtime for Machine Learning (Databricks Runtime ML) with a version higher than 10.3

- Notebooks from *Chapter 9* imported into the Databricks workspace
- Introductory knowledge of hypothesis testing and interpreting statistical tests

Let's take a look at the motivation behind why model monitoring is important.

The motivation behind model monitoring

According to an article in Forbes magazine by Enrique Dans, July 21, 2019, 87% of data science projects never make it to production (`https://www.forbes.com/sites/enriquedans/2019/07/21/stop-experimenting-with-machine-learning-and-start-actually-usingit/?sh=1004ff0c3365`).

There are a lot of reasons why ML models fail; however, if we look purely at the reason for ML project failure in a production environment, it comes down to a lack of re-training and testing the deployed models for performance consistency over time.

The performance of the model keeps degrading over time. Many data scientists neglect the maintenance aspect of the models post-production. The following visualizations offer a comparative analysis between two distinct approaches to model management—one where the model is trained once and then deployed for an extended period and another where the model undergoes regular retraining with fresh data while being monitored for performance drift:

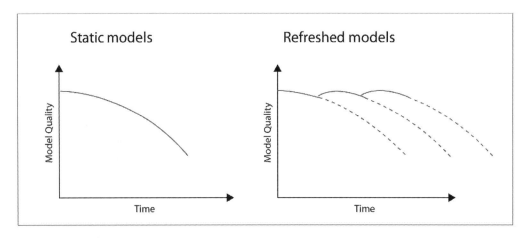

Figure 9.1 – A comparison of model quality for a static model versus a regularly trained model

Source
Courtesy of Databricks

There are a lot of statistical tests that can help us monitor changes in our model's performance over time, and since the field of MLOps is still in the early stages of maturity, ML practitioners struggle with how and which tests to incorporate in their ML productionizing process.

In this chapter, we will dive deeper into what statistical tests we recommend using to monitor ML models in the production environment. Several Python libraries can be seamlessly integrated into the Databricks environment for this purpose. Among these are open source options such as whylogs, Evidently, and Seldon Alibi Detect, which offer various functionalities ranging from data drift tracking to full-scale model health assessments. Although the primary focus of this chapter will be on leveraging statistical tests for model monitoring within Databricks, you are encouraged to explore these libraries to augment your monitoring toolkit. Databricks' flexibility allows you to easily incorporate these libraries into your workflows if you wish to extend beyond statistical approaches.

We will also go over how to use everything we have learned up to now to implement model monitoring on Databricks using open source tools.

The example we'll explore focuses on batch scoring using a tabular dataset. However, the underlying principles are equally applicable to streaming or real-time inference involving image or text data.

Organizations differ in their automation preferences, particularly when it comes to retraining models in response to detected performance drift. In this section, our primary objective is to examine various model monitoring strategies. Depending on your specific use case, you can then determine the most appropriate next steps based on these insights.

To better contextualize where model monitoring fits in, let's examine the typical life cycle of an ML project.

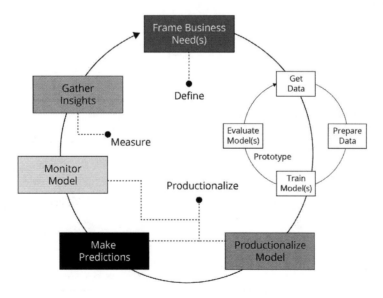

Figure 9.2 – Showing the life cycle of an ML project

> **Source**
> Courtesy of Databricks

The first step in any ML project is the business coming up with a business problem that they believe can benefit from the application of ML. As part of this process, the various stakeholders and the data scientists come up with the online and offline metrics.

Offline metrics are the ones that can be calculated when ML models are being trained, such as accuracy and F1 score. Online metrics are the ones that are business-driven.

After the metrics and success criteria are decided, the data scientists and ML engineers work with the data engineers to understand all the data sources that are available to them and which could be useful for the current business problem. In the preceding figure, this is shown as the **Data Collection** phase.

Once data collection is done, the data scientists proceed to perform the feature engineering and train various ML models, and after evaluating the model, they productionize the best model.

This productionizing of the model is where the model deployment and monitoring come in. The entire process, from collecting data to training and evaluating models and productionizing the best model, is iterative in nature.

Operationalizing the entire process previously explained is what we call MLOps. All the ML deployments look different and depend on the domain and the problem we are trying to solve.

When you are designing your own ML solution on Databricks, spend considerable time determining how often you will train and deploy a new model and what kind of performance monitoring and action will make sense for your use case.

So far, we have discovered that degrading model performance over time is one of the main causes of failed ML projects in organizations. Now, let's take a look at some of the reasons why model performance might degrade over time.

Introduction to model drift

ML models can experience a decline in performance over time, which is a common issue in projects. The main reasons for this are changes in the input data that is fed into the model. These changes can occur due to various reasons, such as the underlying distribution of the data changing, an alteration in the relationship between the dependent and independent features, or changes in the source system that generates the data itself.

The performance degradation of deployed models over time is called Model Drift. To effectively identify instances of Model Drift, various metrics can be monitored:

- **Accuracy**: A declining trend in accuracy can serve as a strong indicator of model drift.

- **Precision and Recall**: A noticeable decrease in these values may highlight the model's diminishing ability to make accurate and relevant predictions.

- **F1 Score**: This is a harmonized metric that encapsulates both precision and recall. A drop in the F1 Score suggests that the model's overall efficacy is compromised.

- **Business Metrics**: Beyond technical indicators, key business metrics like conversion rate, churn rate, and customer lifetime value can also reveal model drift by showing the model's declining impact on business objectives.

There are many categories of model drift, including the following:

- **Feature drift**: Feature drift refers to changes in the distribution of input features or predictors used by an ML model. These changes can occur due to various reasons, such as changes in data collection processes, measurement errors, or shifts in the characteristics of the data source:

  - For example, if a model is trained on data collected from a specific location and time period and then deployed to a different location or time period where the feature distributions are different, the model may experience feature drift. This can result in the degradation of model performance, as the model may not be able to accurately generalize to the new feature distribution.

- **Label drift**: Label drift refers to changes in the distribution of output labels or target variables used for training an ML model. These changes can occur due to shifts in the underlying data generation process, changes in data collection methods, or changes in the definitions of labels:

  - For example, if a model is trained to predict customer churn using historical data and the definition of churn changes over time, the model may experience label drift. This can result in a misalignment between the model's predictions and the ground truth labels, leading to decreased model performance.

- **Prediction drift**: Prediction drift refers to changes in the distribution of model predictions over time. This can occur due to changes in the underlying data distribution, changes in the model's parameters, or changes in the model's architecture:

  - For example, if a model is trained to predict stock prices and deployed in a dynamic financial market, the model's predictions may drift over time as the market conditions change. Prediction drift can impact the reliability and accuracy of the model's predictions, leading to potential business or operational implications.

- **Concept drift**: Concept drift refers to changes in the underlying concepts or relationships between variables in the data distribution over time. This can occur due to changes in the data source, changes in the data generation process, or changes in the underlying phenomenon being modeled:

  - For example, if a model is trained to predict credit risk based on historical credit data and there are changes in the economic or regulatory environment, the model may experience concept drift. Concept drift can result in a misalignment between the model and the real-world phenomenon, leading to decreased model performance.

We can summarize this information on the various types of drift and how to mitigate them as follows:

Types of Drift Encountered	Suggested Steps Upon Drift Identification
Feature Drift	1. Reassess the methods used for feature creation. 2. Revise the data cleaning workflows. 3. Alert the data management team about possible data inconsistencies. 4. Think about updating the model with recent data.
Label Drift	1. Examine the origins of altered labels. 2. Modify the label generation strategy if required. 3. Refresh the model using the newly labeled data. 4. Re-evaluate the model's effectiveness after updates.
Prediction Drift	1. Gauge the effect on key business indicators. 2. Perform an in-depth analysis to identify the root cause. 3. Make model adjustments if the drift is substantial. 4. Keep a close watch to confirm restored stability.
Concept Drift	1. Scrutinize the relationships between features and the target variable. 2. Update the criteria for feature inclusion. 3. Update the model using data that reflects the new relationships. 4. Roll out the revised model and continue to track its performance.

Figure 9.3 – Summarizing the various types of drift and the actions we can perform to mitigate them

Feature drift, label drift, and concept drift collectively fall into the category of **data drift**.

Understanding and addressing drift in ML models is crucial to ensure their continued performance and reliability in real-world applications. Feature drift, label drift, prediction drift, and concept drift are important types of drift that can occur in ML models. Detecting and mitigating drift requires the use of appropriate statistical tests or methods to identify and quantify the changes in data distribution over time.

In the next section, we'll explore another critical factor that can contribute to the deterioration of model performance over time—Statistical Drift.

Introduction to Statistical Drift

Statistical drift refers to changes in the underlying data distribution itself. It can affect both the input features and the target variable. This drift may or may not affect the model's performance but understanding it is crucial for broader data landscape awareness.

To effectively identify instances of Statistical Drift, various metrics can be monitored:

- **Mean and Standard Deviation**: Significant changes can indicate drift.

- **Kurtosis and Skewness**: Changes signal data distribution alterations.

- **Quantile Statistics**: Look at changes in 25th, 50th, and 75th percentiles for example.

To fully grasp how Model Drift and Statistical Drift are interconnected, consider the following key points:

- **Cause and Effect Relationship**: Statistical drift in either the features or the target variable frequently serves as a precursor to model drift. For example, should the age demographic of your customer base shift (indicative of statistical drift), a model designed to predict customer behavior could begin to falter in its performance (resulting in model drift).

- **Simultaneous Occurrence**: Both forms of drift can occur concurrently. Take, for instance, an e-commerce model that experiences model drift due to seasonal variations, while also undergoing statistical drift owing to changes in customer demographics.

- **Diverse Monitoring Requirements**: Each type of drift necessitates its own unique set of monitoring strategies. Model drift is commonly identified through an examination of prediction errors, whereas statistical drift is usually detected by observing shifts in the data distribution.

- **Distinct Corrective Measures**: Addressing model drift typically involves retraining the model or making fine-tuned adjustments. On the other hand, statistical drift may call for more comprehensive changes in data processing protocols or adjustments in feature engineering.

To make an informed decision on which drift detection method to employ, it's essential to weigh the pros and cons of each approach. Your choice will hinge on the specific requirements of your project and the nuances of your business domain. The table below offers a concise summary, highlighting the advantages and challenges of using Model Drift Detection Methods versus Statistical Drift Detection Methods.

Aspect	Model Drift Detection Methods	Statistical Drift Detection Methods
Pros	Ease of detection through performance metrics; Allows for model updates or recalibration	Provides broader understanding of data landscape, Not model-specific
Cons	Requires continual monitoring; Can be resource-intensive	Difficult to quantify; May require sophisticated tests; Less obvious indicators

Table 9.1 – Summarizing the pros and cons of Model Drift Detection
Methods versus Statistical Drift Detection Methods.

In the next section, we will discuss the various techniques we can utilize to monitor drift in our features and model performance over time.

Techniques for drift detection

To ensure effective monitoring of our model's performance over time, we should track changes in summary statistics and distributions of both the model features and target variables. This will enable us to detect any potential data drift early on.

Furthermore, it's important to monitor offline model metrics such as accuracy and F1 scores that were utilized during the initial training of the model.

Lastly, we should also keep an eye on online metrics or business metrics to ensure that our model remains relevant to the specific business problem we are trying to solve.

The following table provides an overview of various statistical tests and methods that can be employed to identify drift in your data and models. Please note that this compilation is not all-encompassing.

Data Type to Monitor	Sub-Category	Statistical Measures and Tests
Numeric Features	Summary Statistics	- Mean
		- Median
		- Minimum
		- Maximum
		- Missing value count

Data Type to Monitor	Sub-Category	Statistical Measures and Tests
	Statistical Tests	- Kolmogorov-Smirnov (KS) test
		- Levene test
		- Wasserstein distance
Categorical Features	Summary Statistics	- Mode
		- Unique level count
		- Missing value count
	Statistical Tests	- Chi-Squared Test
Target-Feature Relation	Numeric Target	- Pearson Coefficient
	Categorical Target	- Contingency Tables
Model Performance	Regression Models	- Mean Square Error (MSE)
		- Error distribution plots
	Classification Models	- Confusion Matrix
		- Accuracy

Table 9.2 – Monitoring table for detecting various types of drift

Going into detail for each and every statistical test is out of the scope of this book. We will be using open source libraries to perform these tests and detect drift; however, it is still beneficial to learn the high-level steps involved in performing some of the tests we will use in the sample notebooks accompanying this chapter.

Let's first understand the basics of hypothesis testing. All statistical tests use the hypothesis testing framework.

Hypothesis testing

When it comes to drawing conclusions about population characteristics based on sample data, hypothesis tests are invaluable. This statistical technique is designed to examine whether meaningful discrepancies exist between distinct sets of data. Let's take a look at the core steps involved in hypothesis testing.

Core steps in hypothesis testing

There are four core steps in hypothesis testing:

1. **Formulate the hypotheses**:

    I.   **Null Hypothesis H0**: This proposes that no noteworthy differences exist between the datasets.

    II.   **Alternate Hypothesis Ha**: This claims that a significant divergence is present between the datasets.

2. **Establish the level of significance**: Often symbolized by α, this value signifies the likelihood of making an erroneous decision by rejecting the null hypothesis when it's actually true. An α value of 0.05 is commonly chosen, which corresponds to a 5% risk of a Type I error.

3. **Compute the test statistic**: This numerical measure is derived from both the sample data and the null hypothesis. It serves as the basis for determining the validity of the null hypothesis.

4. **Ascertain the p-value**: The p-value quantifies the odds of achieving the computed test statistic—or a more extreme result if the null hypothesis holds. This metric guides the decision to either uphold or reject the null hypothesis.

5. **Making the final decision**

    I.   When the $p-value < \alpha$, the null hypothesis is rejected. The data provides ample evidence to support the claim made by the alternate hypothesis.

    II.   When the $p-value < \alpha$, the null hypothesis is not rejected. The evidence to back the alternate hypothesis is insufficient.

So, now we understand the basics of hypothesis testing. Let's go over the steps for some statistical tests that are utilized in the notebook accompanying this chapter to demonstrate drift detection.

To clearly visualize the outcomes of each numerical test we'll discuss, the accompanying figures will be based on a synthetic dataset. This dataset contains two distinct yet comparable sets of data points, labeled as 'Group 1' and 'Group 2':

Group 1

This ensemble includes 1,000 entries, generated using a Gaussian distribution with a zero mean and a unitary standard deviation. Essentially, it's a prototypical bell-shaped curve centered at zero.

Group 2

This assembly, too, comprises 1,000 entries. However, these are pulled from a Gaussian distribution with a mean value of one and a unit standard deviation. The distribution closely resembles that of Group 1, albeit shifted one unit to the right on the x-axis.

Defining Characteristics

- **Sample Size**: Each of the groups, Group 1 and Group 2, contains an equal number of entries, allowing for a balanced comparison.

- **Distribution Nature**: Both groups follow a Gaussian distribution, although the central values are distinct.

- **Uniform Variance**: The variances for both groups are closely matched, making them appropriate for any tests that hinge on equal variance assumptions.

Statistical tests and measurements for numeric features

In the following section, we delve into an array of statistical techniques that are crucial for understanding and analyzing numeric features in your dataset. We'll explore various tests and metrics that can help you assess the quality, distribution, and relationships of these features, thereby aiding in effective model building and monitoring.

Kolmogorov-Smirnov tests

The **Kolmogorov-Smirnov (KS)** two-sample assessment is a non-parametric method of evaluating whether two separate sets of data originate from identical distributions or if their distributions differ in a statistically meaningful way. This test focuses on comparing the **empirical cumulative distribution functions (ECDFs)** of the two datasets. To perform a KS test for detecting drift in our numeric features, we take the following steps:

1. Formulate hypotheses:

    - **Null hypothesis (H0)**: This hypothesis posits that both datasets come from the same distribution.

    - **Alternative hypothesis (H1)**: This hypothesis argues that the two datasets have statistically different distributions.

2. Choose a significance level (alpha). This is the cut-off point for deciding whether to reject the null hypothesis. Typical alpha values are 0.05 or 0.01.

3. Calculate the test statistics and determine the critical value or p-value from the KS test's critical values table.

4. Make a decision:

    I.   Compare the p-value obtained in *step 3* with the chosen significance level (alpha).

    II. If the p-value is less than alpha, reject the null hypothesis and conclude that the variances of the groups or samples are not equal.

If the p-value is larger than alpha, retain the null hypothesis. This suggests that there's insufficient evidence to say the distributions are different.

The following graph depicts the **Empirical Cumulative Distribution Functions (ECDFs)** for Group 1 and Group 2. The red dashed line indicates the maximum difference between the two ECDFs, quantifying the **Kolmogorov-Smirnov (KS)** statistic. The KS statistic and p-value are presented, offering a statistical measure of the drift between the two groups.

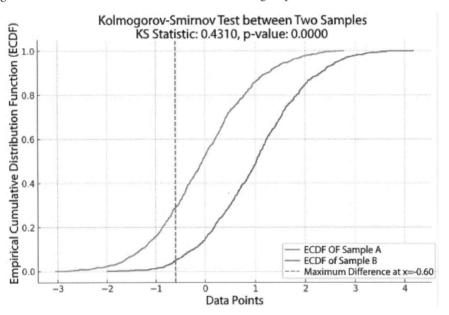

Figure 9.4 – Kolmogorov-Smirnov test visualization using the described dummy data for 'Group 1' and 'Group 2

The KS statistic is 0.4310 and the p-value is nearly 0.0, indicating that the difference between the two groups is statistically significant. In terms of "drift," this suggests that there is indeed a notable change or drift in the distribution between 'Group 1' and 'Group 2.' This is particularly relevant when monitoring models over time for changes in the data they are processing.

It is important to note that, depending on the use case, we may need to use Bonferroni correction to reduce false positives.

Levene t-test

Levene's test is a statistical test used to assess the equality of variances in two or more groups or samples. It is a parametric test that can be used when the assumption of equal variances (homoscedasticity) required by some other tests, such as the t-test or **analysis of variance (ANOVA)**, may not be met. Levene's test can be performed using the following steps:

1.   Formulate the hypotheses:

    •   **Null hypothesis (H0)**: This means the variances of the groups or samples are equal.

    •   **Alternative hypothesis (H1)**: This means the variances of the groups or samples are not equal.

2.   Choose a significance level (alpha).

3.   Calculate the test statistics and compare them to the p-value.

4.   Make a decision:

    I.   Compare the p-value from the third step to the predetermined alpha level.

    II.   If the p-value is smaller than the alpha level, reject the null hypothesis. This indicates that the variances across the groups or samples are not the same.

    III.   If the p-value is larger than the alpha level, retain the null hypothesis. This suggests that there's insufficient evidence to claim the variances are different.

The box plots display the data distributions for 'Group 1' and 'Group 2.' Variances for each group are annotated, and the W statistic and p-value are presented to assess the statistical significance of variance differences.

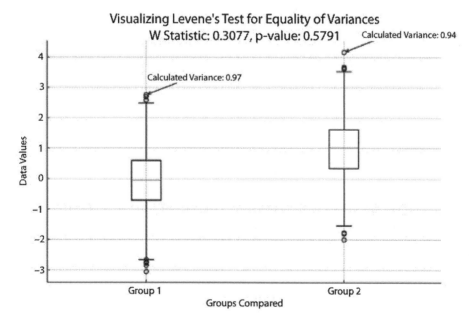

Figure 9.5 – The W statistic and p-value from Levene's test

The W statistic is low, and the p-value is high, suggesting that the variances between the two groups are not significantly different.

Wasserstein distance

Also referred to as the earth mover's distance, the Wasserstein metric serves as a gauge for comparing the likeness or differences between two statistical distributions. It calculates the effort needed to morph one distribution into another, where these distributions can be depicted as histograms or discrete sets of probability values. When it comes to identifying data drift, this metric can be employed to assess how much two distributions diverge from each other, either over time or across varying conditions.

When comparing two distributions using the Wasserstein distance, a higher Wasserstein distance value indicates greater dissimilarity or discrepancy between the distributions, while a lower Wasserstein distance value indicates greater similarity or agreement between the distributions. In the context of data drift detection, an increase in the Wasserstein distance over time or between different environments can indicate the presence of data drift, which refers to changes in the underlying data-generating process or distribution.

In other words, if the Wasserstein distance between two distributions increases significantly over time or between different environments, it suggests that the distributions have diverged and the data may have drifted from the original distribution. This can be an indication of changes in data characteristics, the data-generating process, or the data source. This may prompt further investigation and monitoring to ensure data quality and model performance. The threshold for what constitutes a significant increase in the Wasserstein distance as an indicator of data drift may depend on the specific problem or application. It requires careful consideration and domain knowledge.

The histograms in the following represent the distributions of 'Group 1' and 'Group 2.' The purple dashed lines visually signify the Wasserstein distance, quantifying the amount of 'work' required to transform one distribution into the other.

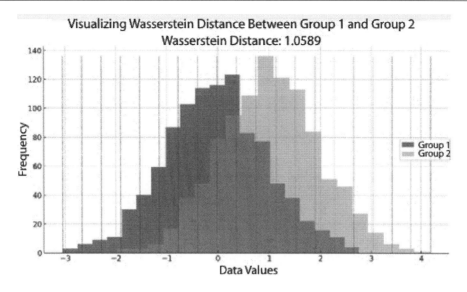

Figure 9.6 – visualization to represent the Wasserstein distance between 'Group 1' and 'Group 2

The Wasserstein distance provides a measure of how much the two distributions differ in terms of their location and shape. In this case, the distance value and the spread of the purple lines across the distributions suggest that there is some level of discrepancy between the two groups, but not an extreme one..

Statistical tests and measurements for categorical features

In this section, we are going to briefly cover one of the most popular tests: the chi-squared test. As mentioned before, all the statistical tests follow the framework of hypothesis testing described in the earlier section.

Chi-squared test

The chi-squared test serves as a statistical method for assessing the presence of a meaningful relationship between two categorical variables, typically represented in a contingency table. The general procedure involves the following steps:

1. Establish the hypotheses:

   - **Null Hypothesis (H0)**: This suggests that no significant relationship exists between the two categorical variables.

   - **Alternative Hypothesis (Ha)**: This indicates that a meaningful relationship does exist between the two categorical variables.

2. **Make the decision**:

   If the chi-squared statistics have a p-value less than the chosen significance level (alpha), we reject the null hypothesis. Otherwise, we accept the null hypothesis.

To offer a clear understanding of the Chi-squared test, we will utilize illustrative visuals based on a synthetic dataset. This dataset comprises two distinct categories, termed 'Group 1' and 'Group 2':

Group *1*

This collection consists of 1,000 entries. Specifically, 572 entries fall under category 'A' and 428 entries under category 'B'.

Group 2

This set also includes 1,000 entries, with 447 entries in category 'A' and 553 entries in category 'B'.

Key Attributes

- **Sample Size**: Both Group 1 and Group 2 have an equal number of entries (N=1,000), enabling a fair comparative analysis.

- **Category Distribution**: Each group contains two categories—'A' and 'B'. However, the distribution of entries across these categories varies between the groups.

- **Uniform Sample Size**: Since both groups have 1,000 entries, they are suitable for statistical tests like the Chi-squared test that benefit from balanced datasets.

The following bar chart showcases the frequencies of categories 'A' and 'B' for 'Group 1' and 'Group 2'. The annotated statistics in the corner provide the calculated Chi-squared statistic, p-value, and degrees of freedom, serving as quantitative measures for the visual comparisons.

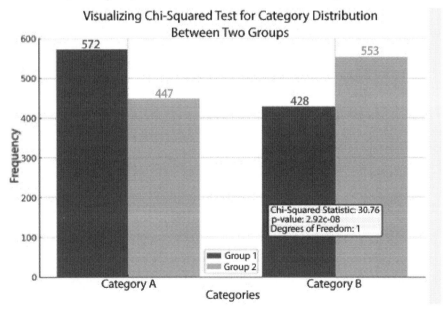

Figure 9.7 – visualization to represent the Chi-squared test results between 'Group 1' and 'Group 2

The extremely low p-value and the high Chi-squared statistic indicate a statistically significant difference between the category distributions of 'Group 1' and 'Group 2'.

For easy reference here's a table detailing various statistical methods, their hypotheses formulation, decision criteria, and example use-cases with metrics.

Method	Formulate Hypotheses	Decision Criteria	Example Metrics	Feature Type
T-Test	Null: Sample means identical | Alt: Sample means differ	Reject null if p-value is less than significance level	Average user session durations: 5 min vs 8 min	Numeric
Chi-Squared Test	Null: No relation between categories | Alt: Categories related	Reject null if p-value is less than significance level	Engagement levels across various ad channels	Categorical
ANOVA	Null: Group averages same | Alt: At least one group average varies	Reject null if p-value is less than significance level	Performance metrics of distinct sales units	Numeric
Kolmogorov-Smirnov Test	Null: Data distributions match | Alt: Data distributions vary	Reject null if D exceeds critical value	Customer age distributions across regions	Numeric
Levene's Test	Null: Equal group variances | Alt: Variances differ between groups	Reject null if p-value is less than significance level	Score variance comparison between genders	Numeric
Wasserstein Distance	Null: Distributions are equal | Alt: Distributions differ	Consider domain-specific threshold for Wasserstein distance	Distributional shift in customer incomes over time	Numeric

Table 9.3 – A guide to statistical methods, their hypotheses, decision criteria, example use-cases, and applicable feature types.

Now we have covered at a high level statistical tests involved for detecting drift for individual features. Let's discuss what monitoring tests we can implement on our models.

Statistical tests and measurements on models

When it comes to monitoring model performance altogether, we can have additional monitoring in place for the following:

- You can monitor the relationship between the target and independent features:

  - **Numeric target**: For calculating and monitoring Pearson coefficients

  - **Categorical target**: For calculating and monitoring contingency tables

- **Model performance**: Here, we can monitor the model's offline metrics over time:

  - **Regression models**: These comprise **Mean square error** (**MSE**), residual plots, **root-mean-squared Error** (**RMSE**), and so on

  - **Classification models**: These comprise accuracy, F1 scores, **receiving operating characteristics** (**ROC**) curves, and so on

  - Tracking performance on holdout datasets

- **Time taken to train**: If the time taken to train the model over time increases drastically, we may need to investigate that

Let's take a look at an end-to-end example of detecting drift on the Databricks platform. We will be working with a synthetic dataset generated to simulate various types of drift.

Implementing drift detection on Databricks

The necessary files for this chapter are located within the `Chapter-09` folder. This example demonstrates how you can arrange your code into specific modules to keep it organized.

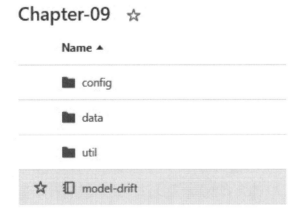

Figure 9.8 – A screenshot showing the layout of the files in our code base

The setup notebook in the `config` folder is designed to establish the folder structure for data reading and writing. It also sets up the MLflow experiment for tracking model performance over time and manages other variables that will be utilized in our `model-drift` notebook.

The `datagen` notebook within the data folder serves the purpose of creating a synthetic dataset that effectively demonstrates the concept of model drift. This dataset encompasses time series data of online sales for an e-commerce website spanning three months.

In this dataset, we have a set of independent features and a target feature, along with simulated relationships between them. The independent features include the following:

- `Temperature` (**Numeric**): This captures the highest daily temperature in Fahrenheit
- `Weather_Condition` (**Categorical**): This variable can have values such as `'sunny'`, `'cloudy'`, or `'rainy'`
- `Promotion_Type` (**Categorical**): This can be classified into categories such as `'discount'`, `'free_gift'`, or `'bundle_deal'`
- `Website_Traffic` (**Numeric**): This represents the total number of visits to the website
- `Device_Type` (**Categorical**): This indicates the type of device used to access the website

The target feature is `Daily_Sales` (numeric), which represents the total sales revenue for each day.

In terms of relationships, the target variable, `Daily_Sales`, has specific correlations with these features. For instance, it shows a **positive correlation** with both `Temperature` and `Website_Traffic`. On the other hand, it has a **negative correlation** with `Weather_Condition` and `Device_Type`.

Our approach involves training the model using the data from the initial month and subsequently simulating diverse drift patterns in the ensuing months' data. This process allows us to effectively explore the impact of changing data distributions and patterns on the model's performance.

Lastly, there are two additional notebooks present inside the `util` folder.

The `monitoring` notebook contains a set of monitoring utility functions designed to ensure the quality and consistency of new incoming data compared to production data in a data-driven environment. These functions cover various aspects, including checking null value proportions, identifying significant differences in summary statistics, detecting variations in variances and distributions, evaluating categorical differences, and comparing model performances. The utility functions assist in maintaining data integrity, identifying potential discrepancies, and providing recommendations for transitioning models to production. Additionally, there's a function to plot boxplots for visualizing distribution differences between incoming and production data.

To perform various statistical tests on data, we are going to use the `scipy.stats` package. The `scipy.stats` package is a fundamental component of the SciPy library, which is widely used in scientific and statistical computing in Python. It provides a comprehensive collection of statistical distributions, functions, and methods for performing various statistical calculations, probability density estimations, and hypothesis testing. With `scipy.stats`, you can easily work with continuous and discrete probability distributions, generate random samples, compute statistical measures, and perform tests to analyze data.

This package encompasses a wide range of statistical techniques, such as calculating probabilities, quantiles, and moments and performing goodness-of-fit tests. The distributions available in `scipy.stats` include common ones such as normal, exponential, uniform, and many more, as well as less common and specialized distributions used in various research fields.

In addition to statistical distributions, `scipy.stats` offers functions for hypothesis testing, correlation analysis, linear regression, and non-parametric tests. You can read more about it on the official website (`https://docs.scipy.org/doc/scipy/reference/stats.html`).

The `training` notebook focuses on training and managing ML models using scikit-learn within the MLflow environment. It includes utility functions for MLflow Model Registry interactions, Delta table-handling, and a detailed ML workflow. The workflow encompasses data loading, preprocessing, training a `RandomForestRegressor` model, evaluating performance, and logging relevant metrics and artifacts to MLflow for model tracking. The script's purpose is to streamline the end-to-end process of training, evaluating, and tracking ML models in a production setting.

With all the supporting notebooks and high-level code explanations out of the way, let's go through the main driver notebook called `model-drift`, which calls all the other notebooks. You can go over the supporting notebooks in your own time.

Let's jump right into the `model-drift` notebook:

1. The initial cells are just calling the other supporting notebooks to have the required libraries, directory structure, raw dataset, and MLflow experiment ready for our example:

```
%run ./config/setup
%run ./util/training
%run ./util/monitoring
%run ./data/datagen
```

2. Next, we use the Databricks notebook widgets to allow us to parametrize our notebook to set certain thresholds for our hypothesis tests and model performance metrics:

```
# Remove all existing widgetsdbutils.widgets.removeAll() #
Create three widgets for the stats threshold limit, p-threshold,
and min model R2 threshold
dbutils.widgets.text("stats_threshold_limit", "0.5")
dbutils.widgets.text("p_threshold", "0.05")
```

```
dbutils.widgets.text("min_model_r2_threshold", "0.005")
# Get the values of the widgets
# stats_threshold_limit: how much we should allow basic summary
stats to shiftstats_threshold_limit = float(dbutils.widgets.
get("stats_threshold_limit"))
# p_threshold: the p-value below which to reject null
hypothesisp_threshold = float(dbutils.widgets.get("p_
threshold"))
# min_model_r2_threshold: minimum model improvementmin_model_r2_
threshold = float(dbutils.widgets.get("min_model_r2_threshold"))
```

3. Ingest the first month's data from the raw synthetic dataset stored as a CSV file into a Delta table:

```
# Ensure we start with no existing Delta table
dbutils.fs.rm(months_gold_path, True) # Incoming Month 1 Data
raw_data = spark.read.csv(raw_good_data_path, header=True,
inferSchema=True)
# Filter the DataFrame to only include data for January 2023
raw_data_month1 = raw_data.filter(raw_data["Date"].
between("2023-01-01", "2023-01-31"))
import pyspark.sql.functions as F
# Create inital version of the Gold Delta table we will use for
training - this will be updated with subsequent "months" of data
raw_data_month1.withColumn("month", F.lit("month_1")).write.
format("delta").mode("overwrite").partitionBy("month").
save(months_gold_path)
```

4. Train the baseline model as an MLflow run using our custom method, `train_sklearn_rf_model`. This run will be available to view under our experiment:

```
# read gold data for month 1 from the Delta table
month1_gold_delta_table = DeltaTable.forPath(spark, path=months_
gold_path)
month1_gold_df = month1_gold_delta_table.toDF()
# Set the month number - used for naming the MLflow run and
tracked as a parameter month = 1
# Specify name of MLflow run
run_name = f"month_{month}"
target_col = "Daily_Sales"
cat_cols = [col[0] for col in month1_gold_df.dtypes if
col[1]=="string" and col[0]!='month']
num_cols= [col[0] for col in month1_gold_df.dtypes if
((col[1]=="int" or col[1]=="double") and col[0]!="Daily_Sales")
]
print(f"category columns : {cat_cols}")print(f"numeric columns :
{num_cols}")
print(f"target column : {target_col}")
```

```
# Define the parameters to pass in the RandomForestRegressor
model
model_params = {"n_estimators": 500,
                "max_depth": 5,
                "max_features": "log2"}
# Define a dictionary of parameters that we would like to use
during preprocessing
misc_params = {"month": month,
               "target_col": target_col,
              "cat_cols": cat_cols,
            "num_cols": num_cols}
# Trigger model training and logging to MLflow
month1_run = train_sklearn_rf_model(run_
name,                           months_gold_path,  model_params,
misc_params)
month_1_run_id = month1_run.info.run_id
```

5. Register the baseline model we trained on the first month's data in the model registry and change its state to production:

```
# Register model to MLflow Model Registry
month_1_model_version = mlflow.register_model(model_uri=f"runs:/
{month_1_run_id}/model", name=mlflow_experiment_name)
# Transition model to Production
month_1_model_version = transition_model(month_1_model_version,
stage="Production")
print(month_1_model_version)
```

6. Let's delve into the run that has been generated as a result of training the baseline model. Locate the flask icon situated on the right-hand side of the notebook and proceed to click on it to access the run. It's important to note that the name of the run might vary given that it is randomly generated.

carefree-boar-104

2023-09-05 13:53:31 ED

⊞ delta_path: ...

⊞ mean_absolute_error_X_t...

Models

sales_pred.../1

Showing 3 runs, for more information go to Experiment UI ☐

Figure 9.9 – A screenshot showing run tracking the baseline model training using the first month's data

In addition to the metrics, our custom model training method contains code that logs the summary statistics of the dataset that we used for training the model.

Figure 9.10 – A screenshot showing the logged summary statistics for the training dataset

7.   Along with this, we also logged the exact version of the Delta table that we used to train the model. This will provide us with reproducibility and lineage in the future if we need to analyze how this model was trained and what features were used to train it.

Figure 9.11 – The logging of the Delta table version and the size
of the training and test sets used for this run

In the rest of the notebook, we simply use this baseline to compare model performance.

8. For the second month's data, we simulate upstream data errors by introducing missing values for `website_traffic` for certain promotion types and changing the measurement of the temperature from Fahrenheit to Celsius. By performing the test that checks the null proportion for all numeric columns, we are able to capture that `web_traffic` has an unusual amount of missing values:

```
print("\nCHECKING PROPORTION OF NULLS.....")
check_null_proportion(month_2_pdf, null_proportion_threshold=.5)
```

```
CHECKING PROPORTION OF NULLS.....
Alert: There are feature(s) that exceed(s) the expected null threshold. Please ensure that the data is ingested correctly
{'Website_Traffic': 0.5357142857142857}

Out[37]: {'Website_Traffic': 0.5357142857142857}

Command took 0.09 seconds -- by ▓▓▓▓▓▓▓▓▓▓▓▓▓ at 9/5/2023, 1:53:09 PM on demo
```

Figure 9.12 – A screenshot showing the results of the null value check on the new data

9. To detect drift in the data, we use the `calculate_summary_stats` method defined in our monitoring notebook to calculate summary statistics on the second month's data. Then, we use the other utility methods, such as `load_summary_stats_pdf_from_run`, to read the summary statistics from our base run to compare the second month's data with:

```
# Incoming Month 2 Data
raw_data_month2 = spark.read.csv(raw_month2_bad_data_path,
header=True, inferSchema=True)
# Filter the DataFrame to only include data for Feb 2023
raw_data_month2 = raw_data_month2.filter(raw_data_
month2["Date"].between("2023-02-01", "2023-02-28"))
# Print the filtered DataFrame
raw_data_month2.show(5)
# Compute summary statistics on new incoming data
# we will keep only the columns that we monitored for the last
mode training data
# convert to pandas dataframe should be used with care as if the
size of data is larger than what can fit on driver node then
this can cause failures.
# In the case of data size being large use proper sampling
technique to estimate population summary statistics.
month_2_pdf = raw_data_month2.toPandas().drop(['Date'], axis=1)
summary_stats_month_2_pdf = calculate_summary_stats(month_2_pdf)
summary_stats_month_2_pdf
# Get the original MLflow run associated with the model
registered under Production
current_prod_run = get_run_from_registered_model(mlflow_
experiment_name, stage="Production")
```

```
# Load in original versions of Delta table used at training time
for current Production model
current_prod_pdf = load_delta_table_from_run(current_prod_run).
toPandas()
# Load summary statistics pandas DataFrame for data which the
model currently in Production was trained and evaluated against
current_prod_stats_pdf = load_summary_stats_pdf_from_
run(current_prod_run, project_local_tmp_dir)
print("\nCHECKING PROPORTION OF NULLS.....")
check_null_proportion(month_2_pdf, null_proportion_threshold=.5)
statistic_list = ["mean", "median", "std", "min", "max"]
unique_feature_diff_array_month_2 = check_diff_in_summary_
stats(summary_stats_month_2_pdf,
current_prod_stats_pdf,
num_cols + [target_col],
stats_threshold_limit,
statistic_list)
unique_feature_diff_array_month_2
```

Our summary statistics comparison tests are able to capture the drift in the data and highlight that the temperature has changed drastically in the new data.

```
CHECKING Temperature.........
    The mean Temperature in the new data is at least 50.0% higher than the mean in the production data. Increased from 27.17 to 76.19.
    The median Temperature in the new data is at least 50.0% higher than the median in the production data. Increased from 27.0 to 74.63.
    The std Temperature in the new data is at least 50.0% higher than the std in the production data. Increased from 5.41 to 11.06.
    The min Temperature in the new data is at least 50.0% higher than the min in the production data. Increased from 12.24 to 56.35.
    The max Temperature in the new data is at least 50.0% higher than the max in the production data. Increased from 36.35 to 97.56.

CHECKING Website_Traffic.........

CHECKING Daily_Sales.........
Out[38]: array(['Temperature'], dtype='<U11')
```

Figure 9.13 – Screenshot showcasing the output generated by the statistical tests comparing the summary statistics between the new month's data and the baseline data

10. Moving forward, we employ the Levine test to assess variations in variance coupled with a corrected Bonferroni test to ascertain statistical significance:

```
print("\nCHECKING VARIANCES WITH LEVENE TEST.....")
check_diff_in_variances(current_prod_pdf, month_2_pdf, num_cols,
p_threshold)
print("\nCHECKING KS TEST.....")
check_dist_ks_bonferroni_test(current_prod_pdf, month_2_pdf,
num_cols + [target_col], p_threshold)
```

11. As the next step in the production stage, you may want to collaborate with the upstream data provider team to understand the root cause of the temperature values have changed so drastically in comparison to our base dataset.

The presented tests serve as illustrative instances, underscoring the seamless integration of drift detection code within your ML workflow on Databricks. It's worth noting that these tests can be effortlessly triggered automatically, mirroring the demonstration in *Chapter 8, Automating ML Workflows Using Databricks Jobs*.

As you progress through the remainder of the notebook, you'll encounter additional examples that illuminate the method of tracking model metrics over time to detect deterioration. Furthermore, you'll gain insights into the programmatic management of model promotion up to the production stage or other stages, a process contingent on the outcomes derived from your tests.

Let's summarize what we learned in this chapter.

Summary

In this chapter, we extensively explored the significance of monitoring both models and data, emphasizing the crucial role of drift detection. Our understanding deepened as we delved into the spectrum of statistical tests at our disposal, which are adept at identifying diverse forms of drift encompassing numerical and categorical features.

Moreover, we engaged in a comprehensive walk-through, exemplifying the application of these concepts. Through a simulated model drift scenario using a synthetic e-commerce dataset, we harnessed the power of various statistical tests from the `scipy.stats` package to accurately pinpoint instances of drift.

As we venture into the next chapter, our focus will pivot toward elucidating the organization within the Databricks workspace and delving into the realm of **continuous integration/continuous deployment (CI/CD)**.

10

Using CI/CD to Automate Model Retraining and Redeployment

Having explored various statistical tests in *Chapter 9*, courtesy of diverse open source libraries on Databricks and their integration with MLflow, we will now focus on an integral component of MLOps on Databricks. In this chapter, we will look at how Databricks unifies DevOps, DataOps, and ModelOps all in a single platform.

In this chapter, we will cover the following topics:

- Introduction to MLOps
- Fundamentals of MLOps and deployment patterns

Let's understand what MLOps is.

Introduction to MLOps

MLOps serves as a multidisciplinary approach that merges the principles of DevOps, ModelOps, and DataOps to facilitate the end-to-end life cycle of ML projects. It aims to streamline the transition from model development to deployment, while also ensuring effective monitoring and management. In this framework, we have the following:

- **DevOps**: This focuses on the continuous integration and deployment of code, aiming for quicker releases and more reliable software
- **ModelOps**: This specializes in managing ML models, ensuring they are effectively trained, validated, and deployed
- **DataOps**: This deals with data management practices, encompassing everything from data collection and preprocessing to storage and analytics

MLOps improves the performance, stability, and long-term efficiency of ML systems. There are two primary risks that MLOps can help mitigate for your use case and industry:

- **Technical risks**: These result from poorly managed models that are not performing as expected. Without MLOps implementing your infrastructure and pipeline to train new models and redeploy them in the production environment, it may be very fragile.

- **Compliance risks**: If you are part of a regulated industry and must keep track of the new regulations and compliances to ensure you are not violating them, MLOps can help mitigate them.

Through automation, MLOps can also reduce and catch errors before getting to the production environment and reduce the time to market to launch and maintain products reliant on the most updated models for your use case.

Now, let's look at Databricks as a platform, which allows you to reduce the risks outlined previously and helps improve the long-term efficiency of your teams and your ML projects.

One unique part of Databricks is that it is a *data-centric AI platform*. As part of this AI platform, Databricks uniquely provides all the necessary components needed to manage the data, models, and code that are part of the ML projects.

To elucidate how Databricks facilitates MLOps, the following figure illustrates the platform's integration capabilities with various tools and services on the Databricks Lakehouse platform:

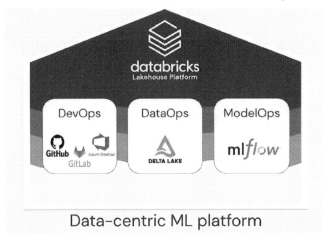

Figure 10.1 – Databricks' data-centric platform and its components

> **Note**
> Courtesy of Databricks.

Next, we'll explore how Delta Lake serves as a pivotal technology that bridges the gap between robust data storage and ML readiness.

Delta Lake – more than just a data lake

When it comes to managing complex data ecosystems, Databricks offers Delta Lake, a comprehensive open source storage layer that we discussed briefly in *Chapter 1*. For more specialized reading, there are other detailed books on this topic, written by my esteemed colleagues, listed in the *Further reading* section of this chapter.

Delta Lake stands out for enhancing the reliability, scalability, and performance of big data processing frameworks, particularly Apache Spark. Developed by Databricks, it equips data lakes with **Atomicity, Consistency, Isolation,** and **Durability** (**ACID**) transactions and robust schema enforcement capabilities. This is particularly crucial because clean and reliable data is not merely an advantage but a prerequisite for any serious data engineering or ML initiative.

Why the need for cleaner data and robust data engineering pipelines?

Having clean data in Delta Lake and robust data engineering pipelines is not just a matter of operational efficiency but a strategic imperative. Data quality directly impacts ML model accuracy, predictive power, and, ultimately, business outcomes. Inconsistent or noisy data can mislead algorithms, leading to incorrect insights and poor decisions. By enforcing strict schema and providing ACID transactions, Delta Lake elevates data lakes from being simple storage repositories to agile, data-ready platforms that can handle the intricacies of ML algorithms effectively.

Efficient pipelines are equally important. They accelerate data flow from the point of ingestion to insights and model deployment. Slow or broken pipelines can bottleneck ML projects, costing organizations both time and money. Delta Lake's transactional capabilities and metadata management help build pipelines that are not just efficient but also resilient and future-proof.

Role of access control in ML modeling

As ML becomes integral to business processes, the requirement for secure and controlled data access intensifies. Delta Lake's **role-based access controls** (**RBACs**) come into play here, integrating seamlessly with organizational identity management systems. This ensures that sensitive data is only accessible to authorized personnel, thereby adding a security layer that helps in meeting regulatory compliance requirements and safeguarding the integrity of ML models.

The key features of Delta Lake include the following:

- **ACID transactions**: Delta Lake ensures atomicity, consistency, isolation, and durability for data operations, allowing concurrent reads and writes. It provides transactional guarantees, so you can confidently perform complex data manipulations.

- **Schema evolution**: Delta Lake supports schema enforcement, allowing you to specify and evolve a schema for your data. It enforces data quality by rejecting writes with incompatible schemas and provides schema evolution capabilities to handle schema changes over time.

- **Time travel**: Delta Lake maintains full historical versions of data, enabling you to query and analyze data at any point in time. You can easily track changes and compare different versions of the data, which is valuable for auditing, debugging, and reproducing analyses.

- **Optimized data processing**: Delta Lake leverages advanced indexing and caching mechanisms to optimize query performance. It uses statistics and optimizations to skip unnecessary data during query execution, resulting in faster response times.

- **Data lake metadata management**: Delta Lake stores metadata in a transaction log, enabling automatic schema discovery and efficient management of table metadata. It provides data lineage information, making it easier to understand the flow and transformation of data.

Delta Lake is highly compatible with Apache Spark, allowing you to leverage Spark's robust analytics capabilities on top of your data lake. It has gained popularity in data lake architectures, enabling data engineers and scientists to build robust, scalable, and reliable data processing pipelines.

Next, let's explore the seamless integration of MLflow within the Databricks platform, which offers robust capabilities for end-to-end model management. We'll also delve into the emerging domain of ModelOps.

Comprehensive model management with Databricks MLflow

For managing models, Databricks provides managed MLflow, which we have already covered in the previous chapters in great depth.

MLflow is an open source platform designed to simplify the ML life cycle. It provides a comprehensive set of tools and APIs for managing, tracking, and deploying ML models. MLflow was developed by Databricks and has gained significant adoption within the ML community.

MLflow consists of four main components:

- **Tracking**: MLflow Tracking allows you to log and track experiments, parameters, metrics, and artifacts associated with your ML projects. It provides a unified interface to record and compare different experiment runs, making it easier to reproduce results and iterate on models. Tracking also supports integration with ML frameworks, such as TensorFlow, PyTorch, and scikit-learn.

- **Projects**: MLflow Projects provides a standard format for packaging and sharing ML code. With MLflow Projects, you can define your ML code as a reusable project, including the code, dependencies, and configuration. This enables reproducibility and collaboration by ensuring your code can be easily executed in different environments.

- **Models**: MLflow Models enables you to manage and deploy ML models in various formats. It provides a simple model format that allows you to package models with their associated metadata and dependencies. You can then deploy these models in various deployment environments, such as batch scoring, real-time serving, or cloud platforms.

- **Model Registry**: MLflow Model Registry is an optional component that adds model versioning, stage transitions, and collaboration features to MLflow Models. It allows you to keep track of different versions of your models, promotes models through different stages (for example, staging to production), and manages access control for different team members.

MLflow supports multiple programming languages, including Python, R, and Java. It can be used both in local development environments and distributed clusters, making it suitable for different deployment scenarios.

As we transition from discussing model management with Databricks MLflow, let's delve into the synergy between DevOps and MLOps, and how these principles are adapted and extended for robust ML pipelines within the Databricks ecosystem.

Integrating DevOps and MLOps for robust ML pipelines with Databricks

Databricks integrates with well-known Git providers such as GitHub, GitLab, and Azure DevOps for managing and executing DevOps workflows for our ML projects.

DevOps combines software **development (Dev)** and IT **operations (Ops)** to foster collaboration, automation, and continuous delivery. It aims to streamline software systems' development, deployment, and maintenance.

By incorporating DevOps principles, MLOps brings an added layer of efficiency to the life cycle of ML models. It fosters cohesive collaboration across every stage of the process – from developing and validating models to their deployment, monitoring, retraining, and redeployment.

Within the sphere of MLOps, **continuous integration and continuous delivery (CI/CD)** emerge as critical elements. They underpin automation and drive continuous learning within ML systems. The ultimate goal of CI/CD is to seamlessly integrate data with source code versions, execute parallel tasks initiated by pertinent events, compile artifacts, and propagate releases to the production stage.

Continuous learning through combining CI and CD principles is essential for the success of an ML system. Without it, the system risks stagnation and becoming a fruitless **Proof of Concept (POC)**. Consistent learning and adaptation enable an ML model to provide valuable business insights.

To use ML models that continually improve, you need to understand CI, CD, and related methods. They work together and depend on each other, as shown in *Figure 10.2*:

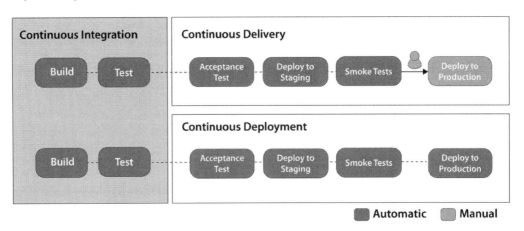

Figure 10.2 – The relationship between continuous integration,
continuous delivery, and continuous deployment

Let's understand these methods in a bit more detail:

- **Continuous integration**: In MLOps, CI is not merely about testing and validating code but also extends to testing and validating data, data schemas, and ML models. This ensures a more robust and reliable integration process tailored to ML needs.

- **Continuous delivery**: Beyond deploying a single software package or service, CD in an MLOps context is about deploying an entire system, which often includes an ML training pipeline and a model prediction service.

- **Continuous deployment**: Similar to traditional DevOps, CD in MLOps goes one step further by fully automating the release process and deploying new changes to production without human intervention.

- **Continuous training**: Unique to ML systems, CT focuses on automatically retraining and serving models, ensuring they adapt and improve over time.

At the time of writing this book, Databricks is working on a new feature called the MLOps Stack, which provides a template to structure complex ML projects for CI/CD integration with Git providers.

For further details regarding the MLOps Stack, you are encouraged to peruse *MLOps Stack* on GitHub (`https://github.com/databricks/mlops-stack`).

We will not be covering the MLOps Stack in this chapter; instead, we will cover another approach to building your MLOps pipelines on Databricks based on utilizing what we have learned so far.

Let's dive deeper and understand the fundamentals of MLOps and the various deployment paradigms.

Fundamentals of MLOps and deployment patterns

To effectively manage MLOps, it's essential to first familiarize ourselves with its underlying terminology and structure. This includes understanding the roles and responsibilities associated with various operational environments – namely, **development (dev)**, staging, and **production (prod)**. Let's dissect what these environments signify in a practical MLOps framework.

Within any ML project, there are three pivotal assets:

- **Code base**: This serves as the project's blueprint. It contains all the source code related to data preprocessing, model training, evaluation, and deployment.

- **Data**: This includes the datasets that are used for training, validating, and testing the model. The quality and availability of this data directly influence the model's efficacy.

- **Trained model**: This is the culmination of your ML workflow, a model that has been trained, evaluated, and prepared for inference.

Each of these assets goes through distinct phases – development, testing, and deployment – which are often segregated into separate environments:

- **Development environment (dev)**: This is where the initial code is written and tested. It's generally the most accessible in terms of code and data but has the least stringent quality and testing requirements.

- **Staging environment**: This serves as an intermediate space for additional testing and quality assurance before the project moves to production.

- **Production environment (prod)**: This is the most restrictive environment where the finalized assets are deployed. It has the highest quality and security requirements and is the least accessible for direct interactions. The following figure provides a visual representation of the key assets in MLOps, as well as the organizational structure of different environments. It illustrates the life cycle of these assets as they progress through development, testing, and, ultimately, production:

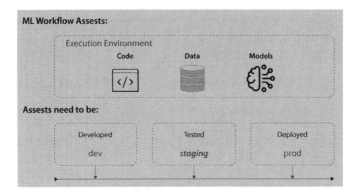

Figure 10.3 – The various assets related to an ML project and its environments

> **Note**
> The preceding figure is courtesy of Databricks.

The following figure illustrates the accessibility levels and quality requirements across these environments:

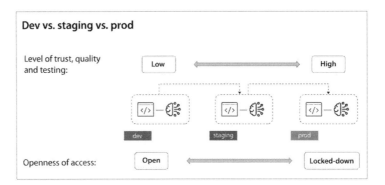

Figure 10.4 – The various environments and their openness to accessibility

> **Note**
> The preceding figure is courtesy of Databricks.

With Databricks, you have the flexibility to structure these dev, staging, and prod environments in various ways to meet your project's specific needs.

It's important to note that the theoretical separation of dev, staging, and prod environments serves as a guideline for best practices in MLOps. However, the real-world implementation can vary significantly based on your organizational needs, workflow, and technological capabilities.

In the following section, we will delve into multiple approaches for deploying Databricks workspaces to better align your dev, staging, and prod environments with your specific organizational requirements.

The following figure showcases three distinct deployment patterns designed to set up your dev, QA, and prod environments effectively:

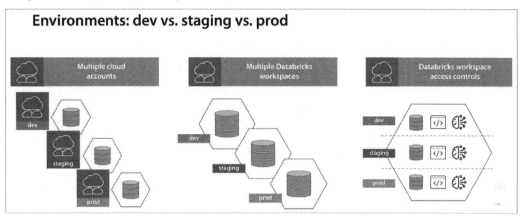

Environments: dev vs. staging vs. prod

Figure 10.5 – Various Databricks environment deployment approaches

> **Note**
> This is the source for the preceding figure: *The Big Book of MLOps*.

Let's understand these patterns one by one.

Navigating environment isolation in Databricks – multiple strategies for MLOps

To devise a robust MLOps strategy, you need to consider not only the type of assets involved but also the environment where they reside – dev, staging, or prod. Each environment offers varying levels of accessibility, testing rigor, and data security, informed by organizational size, governance policies, and security requirements.

Multiple cloud accounts

For large organizations governed by stringent rules and regulations, separating dev, staging, and prod environments across distinct cloud accounts is a common practice. In such a setup, each cloud account will host its own Databricks workspace. This architecture ensures isolation at both the cloud account and network levels, while also potentially increasing costs due to duplicated resources and data storage.

A single cloud account with multiple Databricks workspaces

Alternatively, smaller organizations or projects may opt for a single cloud account containing multiple Databricks workspaces. Each workspace is deployed into its own network and is isolated at that level. While more cost-effective, this approach still allows for sufficient isolation and can align well with organizational data governance policies.

A single cloud account with a single Databricks workspace

Even within a single cloud account, Databricks provides the capability to enforce strict isolation between different roles and projects. Features such as RBAC, permissions, and native data governance tools such as Unity Catalog allow for effective segregation of access within a single workspace.

Having explored various approaches for organizing our dev, staging, and prod environments in Databricks, it's time to turn our attention to another pivotal aspect of MLOps: the asynchronous nature of life cycles in ML projects. This stands in contrast to traditional software DevOps, where code and application updates usually happen in lockstep.

Consider a deployed **large language model** (**LLM**) as a case in point. The sheer complexity and size of such models can make retraining a formidable challenge. You may find that while the data engineering code sees monthly iterations, the training code for the model itself remains static for an extended duration.

On the flip side, think about a churn prediction model. Here, automatic retraining might be scheduled monthly using fresh datasets. If the newly trained model outperforms its predecessor, it immediately gets moved to production, all without requiring any changes to the existing code base.

Navigating asynchronous life cycles

Given the incongruent update cycles for ML models and code, adopting strategies to manage these asynchronicities becomes imperative. You might employ techniques such as canary deployments for safer model rollouts, or opt for blue-green deployments to ensure smoother rollbacks. Automated monitoring systems and alert mechanisms are equally important, serving as early warning systems for model degradation or operational issues, thus allowing for quick remediation.

Fiscal and regulatory considerations

Beyond technical aspects, MLOps also encompasses financial and compliance variables. Cost considerations can't be overlooked – both for data storage and computational resources. Furthermore, data lineage is essential for keeping tabs on data movement through your pipeline, which not only aids in debugging but is invaluable for compliance and auditing purposes. Similarly, data versioning is indispensable when it comes to model reproducibility, an especially crucial feature for models undergoing frequent retraining.

With this nuanced understanding, we are better equipped to manage the complexities that arise from asynchronous updates in the ML life cycle, in the context of Databricks or any MLOps platform.

Now, let's take a look at the various ML deployment paradigms that you can utilize.

Understanding ML deployment patterns

The ultimate goal of any ML project is to get our ML model into production. Depending on what kind of use case we are catering to and how sophisticated our ML engineering team is, there are two broad ML deployment approaches:

- The deploy models approach
- The deploy code approach

Let's understand these approaches one by one.

The deploy models approach

The model deployment workflow adheres to a structured methodology, beginning in a development environment where code for training the ML model is both crafted and refined. After the model undergoes training and the optimal version is ascertained, it is formally registered within a specialized model registry. This is followed by a battery of integration tests to evaluate its performance and reliability. Upon successfully passing these assessments, the model is first elevated to a staging environment for further validation. Once it meets all requisite criteria, it is then deployed into the production environment.

The following figure offers a graphical depiction of this multi-stage approach:

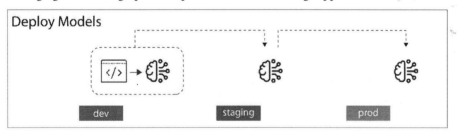

Figure 10.6 – The deploy models approach

> **Note**
> This is the source for the preceding figure: *The Big Book of MLOps*.

Throughout this book, all the notebooks we have utilized so far focus on this particular deployment approach. It is a popular choice among companies and teams, especially when the ML team comprises individuals with a background in data science rather than traditional software engineering. This approach offers simplicity and serves as a great starting point for ML projects.

The following figure showcases the entire end-to-end MLOps life cycle for the deploy models approach:

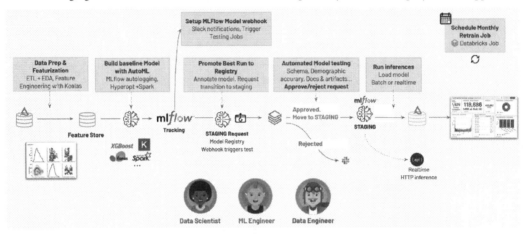

Figure 10.7 – The reference architecture and workflow for deploying a model
from development to production using the deploy models approach

> **Note**
> The preceding figure is courtesy of Databricks.

In this MLOps workflow, data engineers, data scientists, and ML engineers collaborate to perform various steps to ensure the successful development, deployment, and monitoring of ML models. Here is a breakdown of the responsibilities and tasks performed by each role:

- **Data engineers**:

  - Collect data from diverse sources such as databases, cloud storage, and sensors, ensuring reliability and quality

  - Cleanse and preprocess the data, handling tasks such as removing duplicates, handling missing values, and transforming data into a format suitable for ML algorithms

  - Store and manage data in a data warehouse or Delta Lake, ensuring accessibility and efficient utilization by data scientists and ML engineers

- **Data scientists**:

  - Explore and analyze the data to gain insights into its characteristics, identifying relevant patterns and relationships.

  - Generate and register features into feature tables for reuse.

  - Develop and train ML models, employing various algorithms and techniques to achieve accurate predictions and desired outcomes. All the model runs and experiments are logged automatically into the MLflow tracking server on Databricks.

  - Evaluate and assess the performance of the trained models using appropriate metrics and validation techniques.

  - Select the most suitable model for deployment based on performance and business requirements. The best model is then registered in the Model Registry as a candidate model.

- **ML engineers**:

  - Deploy ML models into production environments, making them available for making predictions or decisions in real time

  - Monitor the performance of deployed models, ensuring they operate optimally and detect any anomalies or drift in their behavior

  - Update and retrain models as new data becomes available, maintaining model relevance and accuracy

All the notebooks that we covered as part of this book show this workflow.

Now that we understand how the deploy models approach for MLOps works, let's take a look at the deploy code approach.

The deploy code approach

In the deploy code approach, we version control not only the code to train the ML models but also the code to create the feature tables. This approach works well when you have strict regulations to separate data access in each environment.

The data scientists develop code in the dev environment for feature engineering and model training. After a good candidate model is found, the dev branch code is committed to the staging branch, where automated unit tests are run. Again, we train the model in staging and perform our performance benchmark test. Once everything else looks good, we push the code to the main branch and the prod environment. Here, again, we retrain the model on the data in production:

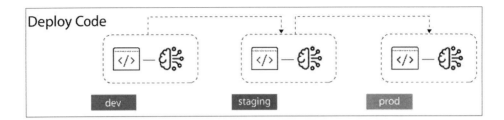

Figure 10.8 – The reference architecture and workflow for deploying a model
from development to production using the deploy code approach

> **Note**
>
> This is the source for the preceding figure: *The Big Book of MLOps*.

The development process involves several stages, starting with the creation of code for the training model and feature engineering in the dev environment. The following figure showcases the deploy code workflow step by step in the dev environment:

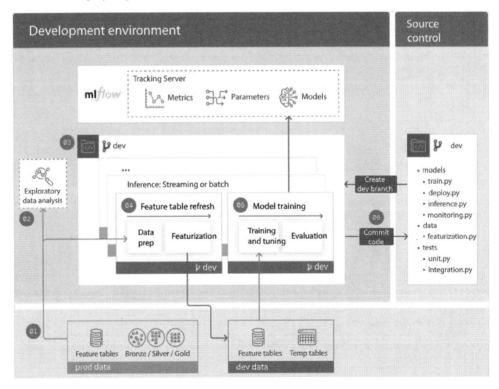

Figure 10.9 – The deploy code workflow within the development environment

> **Note**
>
> Courtesy of Databricks

Let's understand these steps one by one:

1. **Data access points**: In development settings, data scientists typically have read-only permissions for production data. For compliance reasons, access may be limited to sanitized or duplicate versions of this data. A separate development storage is also available for read-write operations, facilitating experimental work.

2. **Preliminary data investigation (PDI)**: Data scientists use an iterative, interactive method for data exploration, leveraging notebooks, visual charts, and Databricks SQL. This step is often a standalone process and not usually part of deployable pipelines.

3. **Source code management**: All ML system code resides in a version control repository. Data scientists work on a development branch within this Git repository. Code can be synchronized with the Databricks workspace via Databricks Repos.

4. **Enhance feature datasets**: This pipeline ingests data from both raw and existing feature tables, outputting it to tables within Feature Store. This step includes two main tasks:

   I.   **Quality assurance**: Here, the data is validated to ensure it meets quality standards.

   II. **Feature construction**: Code is written or updated by data scientists to generate new features. Data may be pulled from Feature Store or other Lakehouse tables. These dev feature tables are used to build experimental models, and upon promotion to production, they update the corresponding production tables.

   Management can be separate for feature pipelines if they are governed by different teams.

5. **Model training pipeline**: Data scientists build pipelines for model training on either read-only production data or development-specific data. These pipelines may utilize feature tables from both the dev and prod environments:

   I.   **Tuning and training**: The training process sources data from feature stores and varying levels of Lakehouse tables while logging parameters, metrics, and artifacts in the MLflow tracking system.

   II. **Model storing**: After training and tuning have been finalized, the model is stored on the MLflow tracking server, capturing its association with the input data and the code.

   When executed in staging or production, the model can be retrieved and registered for ongoing management and testing.

6. **Code finalization**: Once the development work on pipelines for features, training, and inference is complete, either the data scientist or the ML engineer commits these changes to the version control system from the development branch.

Let's move on and understand the workflow in the staging environment. The staging environment serves as the final testing ground for ML code before it transitions to production. It encompasses comprehensive testing of all pipeline components, including model training and feature engineering. ML engineers employ a CI pipeline to execute unit and integration tests. Successful completion results in a release branch, triggering the CI/CD system to initiate the production stage.

The following diagram provides a step-by-step visual guide to the workflow within the staging environment:

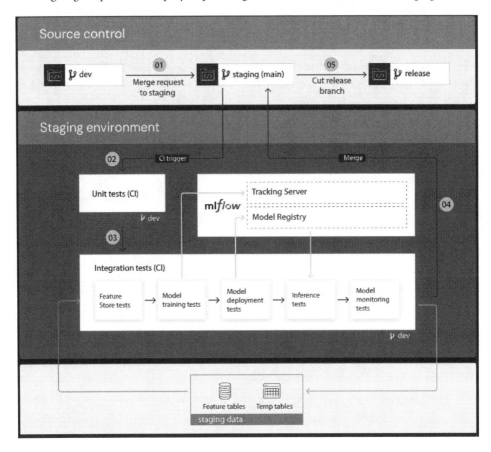

Figure 10.10 – The deploy code workflow within the staging environment

> **Note**
> Courtesy of Databricks

Let's delve into each of these steps in detail:

1. **Initiate merge process**: The journey toward deployment commences when an ML engineer submits a merge request to the source control's staging branch, often the "main" branch. This action sets off a **CI** workflow.

2. **Execute unit tests**: Within the CI framework, the source code is automatically compiled, and unit tests are initiated. Should these tests not succeed, the merge request gets dismissed. Note that unit tests operate in isolation from data or external services.

3. **Conduct integration tests**: Following the unit tests, the CI mechanism proceeds to administer integration tests. These tests validate the compatibility and functionality of all pipelines, which encompasses feature engineering, model training, inference, and monitoring. The staging environment is designed to mirror the production setting as closely as feasible.

   To economize on test duration, concessions may be made between the thoroughness of testing and execution speed. For instance, smaller data subsets could be used, or fewer training cycles run. Depending on the model's intended application, comprehensive load testing might be conducted at this stage.

   After successful completion of integration tests in the staging branch, the code becomes eligible for production deployment.

4. **Commit to the staging branch**: Should the tests be successful, the code merges into the staging branch. In case of test failure, the CI/CD system alerts the relevant parties and updates the merge (or pull) request with the results.

   Periodic integration tests can be scheduled on the staging branch, especially if it receives frequent updates from multiple contributors.

5. **Establish a release branch**: Once the code has been validated and is ready for production deployment, the ML engineer forms a release branch. This action prompts the CI/CD system to refresh the production tasks.

Lastly, let's understand the production environment's workflow.

In the production environment, ML engineers oversee the deployment of ML pipelines that handle feature computation, model training, and testing, as well as prediction publishing and performance monitoring. A retraining mechanism operates on production data to keep the model up to date and optimized. Performance benchmarks are rigorously evaluated to ensure that the new model meets or exceeds the set standards. Data scientists typically lack write and compute permissions in this environment but maintain visibility into test outcomes, logs, model artifacts, and pipeline statuses to aid in diagnosing any production issues.

The following diagram offers a comprehensive, step-by-step visualization of the workflow processes in the production environment:

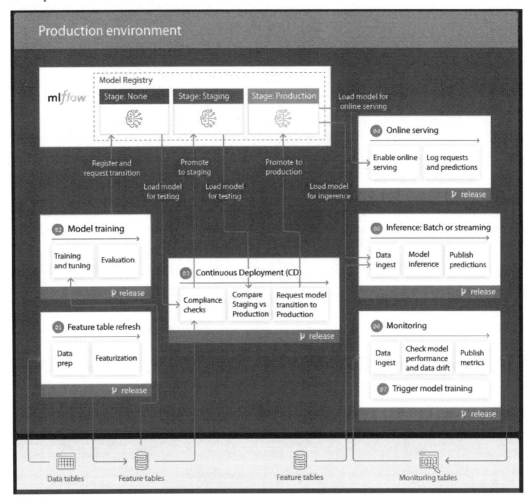

Figure 10.11 – The deploy code workflow within the production environment

> **Note**
> Courtesy of Databricks

Let's go through this workflow step by step:

1. **Refresh feature data**: This phase involves ingesting new data from production and updating tables in Feature Store. This can be either a batch or real-time process and can be invoked by different triggers, such as schedules or continuous runs.

2. **Model training**:

   • **Tuning and training**: The pipeline trains the production model on complete data and logs relevant metrics and parameters through autologging. Unlike the development stage, only top-performing algorithms and hyperparameters are considered to optimize time and performance.

   • **Model assessment**: The quality of the model is tested against a separate dataset from production. Test results and custom metrics are recorded.

   • **Model registration**: Upon successful training, the model is registered with an initial status of "None" in Model Registry.

3. **Automated deployment**:

   • **Compliance verification**: The pipeline performs mandatory compliance checks, which can include human review for complex evaluations. The results are logged.

   • **Performance validation**: Models in the staging phase are compared against those in production to avert performance decay.

   • **Transition to production**: The model is advanced to the production stage, either manually or automatically, following satisfactory performance comparisons.

4. **Real-time serving**: MLflow enables the model to be deployed for low-latency use cases. The deployed model fetches features and returns predictions for each incoming request.

5. **Batch or stream inference**: For higher throughput or latency requirements, batch or stream-based inferences are processed. Predictions can be saved in various storage options, including message queues such as Apache Kafka.

6. **Ongoing monitoring**:

   • **Data feeding**: Logs from different inference types are ingested

   • **Performance and drift metrics**: Various quality and performance metrics are calculated

   • **Metric reporting**: Metrics are saved for further analysis and alerting purposes

7. **Retraining triggers**: Models can be automatically retrained based on a schedule or triggered by performance degradation.

> **Note**
>
> Automating the retraining process can be complex and may require manual intervention to resolve issues identified through monitoring, such as data drift or performance degradation.

The following figure summarizes the various steps that are performed in various environments for the deploy code approach to ModelOps:

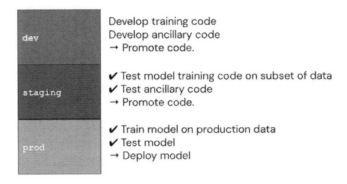

Figure 10.12 – The various steps performed in various environments
for the deploy code approach to ModelOps

> **Note**
>
> The preceding figure is courtesy of Databricks.

Overall, you have three environments. At the top, you have your Git workflow provider, which manages transitioning code from one environment to another. At the bottom, you have the data access layer or feature tables with data across different environments.

The important point to keep in mind here is that the trained model itself will have its own stages in Model Registry in the production environment. We retrain the model again in each environment and hydrate the respective feature tables based on the updated code.

> **Note**
>
> This approach may resonate more with individuals who have a background in traditional software engineering and are acquainted with DevOps principles. However, at the time of writing this book, there is no officially established method for implementing the deploy code approach of MLOps on the Databricks platform using the currently generally available tools. Although we discussed the concepts of the deploy code approach in this section, we won't be covering this as part of the provided code.

MLOps Stack is going to address this model deployment paradigm when it becomes generally available. We will update this book once the new feature is available.

Now, let's wrap up this chapter and summarize our key learnings.

Summary

In this chapter, we covered the basics of MLOps, the different deployment approaches on Databricks, and their reference architectures.

Selecting a model deployment approach should be based on your team's proficiency in implementing DevOps processes for ML projects. It's important to acknowledge that there is no universal solution as each approach we have discussed has its own advantages and disadvantages. However, it is possible to create a customized hybrid ModelOps architecture within the Databricks environment.

By considering your team's strengths and expertise, you can determine the most suitable deployment approach for your project. It's essential to assess scalability, maintainability, ease of deployment, and integration with existing infrastructure. Evaluating these aspects will help you make an informed decision and optimize the model deployment process.

In Databricks, you have the flexibility to tailor your ModelOps architecture to your project's requirements. Leveraging the capabilities of Databricks, you can combine the best elements from different deployment approaches to create a customized and efficient workflow. This hybrid approach allows you to leverage the strengths of different methodologies while mitigating their limitations.

Remember, the ultimate goal is to establish a robust and streamlined model deployment process that aligns with your team's capabilities and project needs. By carefully considering your options and utilizing the resources in the Databricks environment, you can create a ModelOps architecture that maximizes efficiency and productivity for your ML projects.

Further reading

Please go through the following sources and their links to learn more about the topics that were covered in the chapter:

1. *The Big Book of MLOps*: `bit.ly/big-book-of-mlops`

2. *MLOps Stack on GitHub*: `https://github.com/databricks/mlops-stack`

3. Damji, J. S., Wenig, B., Das, T., and Lee, D. (2020). *Learning Spark* (2nd ed.)

Index

Symbols

%pip
  utilizing, in notebooks to install
    notebook-scoped libraries 42, 43

A

access
  managing, in Model Registry 100-110
algorithms
  supported, by Databricks AutoML 79
Amazon Simple Storage Service (S3) 4
Amazon Web Service (AWS) 14, 20
analysis of variance (ANOVA) 175
Apache Spark 12, 49
application programming interface (API) 64
**area under the receiver operating
    characteristic curve (AUC-ROC) 66**
artificial intelligence (AI) 10
**Atomicity, Consistency, Isolation,
    and Durability (ACID) 14, 193**
automatic logging (autolog) capabilities 66
AutoML 77
  need for 78

reference link 38, 95
running, on churn prediction dataset 83-95
Azure Data Lake Storage (ADLS) 4

B

Bank Customer Churn 99
batch inference 49
  ML models, deploying for 122
  performing, on Databricks 122-124
built-in model flavors, MLflow
  reference link 39
business intelligence (BI) 14

C

California Privacy Rights Act (CCPA) 8
candidate model
  registering, to Model Registry 100-110
change data capture (CDC) 5
chi-squared test 177-179
  key attributes 178
churn prediction dataset
  AutoML, running on 83-95
clean data
  need for 193

M

Packtpub.com

Subscribe to our online digital library for full access to over 7,000 books and videos, as well as industry leading tools to help you plan your personal development and advance your career. For more information, please visit our website.

Why subscribe?

- Spend less time learning and more time coding with practical eBooks and Videos from over 4,000 industry professionals

- Improve your learning with Skill Plans built especially for you

- Get a free eBook or video every month

- Fully searchable for easy access to vital information

- Copy and paste, print, and bookmark content

Did you know that Packt offers eBook versions of every book published, with PDF and ePub files available? You can upgrade to the eBook version at packtpub.com and as a print book customer, you are entitled to a discount on the eBook copy. Get in touch with us at customercare@packtpub.com for more details.

At www.packtpub.com, you can also read a collection of free technical articles, sign up for a range of free newsletters, and receive exclusive discounts and offers on Packt books and eBooks.

Other Books You May Enjoy

If you enjoyed this book, you may be interested in these other books by Packt:

Machine Learning for Emotion Analysis in Python

Allan Ramsay, Tariq Ahmad

ISBN: 978-1-80324-068-8

- Distinguish between sentiment analysis and emotion analysis
- Master data preprocessing and ensure high-quality input
- Expand the use of data sources through data transformation
- Design models that employ cutting-edge deep learning techniques
- Discover how to tune your models' hyperparameters
- Explore the use of naive Bayes, SVMs, DNNs, and transformers for advanced use cases
- Practice your newly acquired skills by working on real-world scenarios

Machine Learning with LightGBM and Python

Andrich van Wyk

ISBN: 978-1-80056-474-9

- Get an overview of ML and working with data and models in Python using scikit-learn
- Explore decision trees, ensemble learning, gradient boosting, DART, and GOSS
- Master LightGBM and apply it to classification and regression problems
- Tune and train your models using AutoML with FLAML and Optuna
- Build ML pipelines in Python to train and deploy models with secure and performant APIs
- Scale your solutions to production readiness with AWS Sagemaker, PostgresML, and Dask

Packt is searching for authors like you

If you're interested in becoming an author for Packt, please visit `authors.packtpub.com` and apply today. We have worked with thousands of developers and tech professionals, just like you, to help them share their insight with the global tech community. You can make a general application, apply for a specific hot topic that we are recruiting an author for, or submit your own idea.

Share Your Thoughts

Now you've finished *Practical Machine Learning on Databricks*, we'd love to hear your thoughts! Scan the QR code below to go straight to the Amazon review page for this book and share your feedback or leave a review on the site that you purchased it from.

`https://packt.link/r/1-801-81203-9`

Your review is important to us and the tech community and will help us make sure we're delivering excellent quality content.

Download a free PDF copy of this book

Thanks for purchasing this book!

Do you like to read on the go but are unable to carry your print books everywhere? Is your eBook purchase not compatible with the device of your choice?

Don't worry, now with every Packt book you get a DRM-free PDF version of that book at no cost.

Read anywhere, any place, on any device. Search, copy, and paste code from your favorite technical books directly into your application.

The perks don't stop there, you can get exclusive access to discounts, newsletters, and great free content in your inbox daily

Follow these simple steps to get the benefits:

1. Scan the QR code or visit the link below

https://packt.link/free-ebook/9781801812030

2. Submit your proof of purchase
3. That's it! We'll send your free PDF and other benefits to your email directly

Made in the USA
Monee, IL
27 June 2024

60701505R00136